MW01142361

Investigating Properties and Interactions of Compounds

J.Hemalatha

CONTENT

CHAPTER- I

A PROLOGUE TO THE THESIS WORK

1. INTRODUCTION

Flavonoids belong to a massive institution of considerable plant secondary metabolites, which may be determined in vascular plant life along with ferns, conifers, and flowering plant life [1]. These compounds are usually divided into diverse instructions on the premise of their molecular systems together with chalcones, flavones, flavanones, flavanols, and anthocyanidins. Approximately, 4000 kinds of flavonoids had been recognized and lots of those are excessive pigments, imparting a spectrum of yellow, red, and blue colorings in flowers, fruits, and leaves [2]. Besides their contribution to plant color, flavonoids have numerous pharmacological advantages and are referred to as powerful antioxidants [3]. Natural and artificial flavonoids are consequently of large hobby in the improvement of novel healing retailers for diverse sicknesses and are usually believed to be non-poisonous compounds when you consider that they may be broadly disbursed in the human diet. Prehistoric healing packages may be related to the thousand-year-antique use of plant life and herbs for the remedy of various scientific disorders. Contemporary research records a beneficent variant of massive pharmacological activity.

Among the herbal merchandise remoted from plant life, flavonoids constitute one of the maximum vital and exciting instructions of biologically lively compounds. Chalcones are not unusual place precursors to the flavonoids own circle of relatives and show off a massive wide variety of various organic sports [4]. In the closing 15 years, chalcones have emerged as capacity anticancer retailers [5].

The chemical shape of a flavonoid may be visualized as benzene ring that are linked through a quick carbon chain. For all subclasses of flavonoids, besides chalconoids, the fast chain is hooked up to one of the benzene rings, both without delay or via an oxygen bridge, thereby forming a five-membered ring [6]. As such, flavonoids had been the point of interest in several fundamental biomedical research in addition to medical investigation. For example, excessive nutritional consumption of flavonoids might also additionally provide the capacity to lessen the danger of diverse cancers in line with some the epidemiological research. In addition, flavonoids had been pronounced to show a wide spectrum of pharmacological sports [7].

1.1 CHALCONES

Chalcones were first synthesized in the laboratory in the late 1800s while naturally occurring chalcones were not isolated until 1910 [8]. The time-period chalcone derives from the Greek chalcos which means bronze [9]. Chalcones are a collection of phenolic or flavonoid compounds broadly disbursed in the plant kingdom [10]. Chalcones are open-chain flavonoids wherein the two fragrant phenyl rings are joined through an α,β-unsaturated enone system [11]. Chalcones, or 1,3-diaryl-2-propen-1-ones, belong to the flavonoids own circle of relatives. Compounds with heterocyclic ring structures are becoming of plenty of greater significance in medicinal and commercial fields [12]. Chalcone is a flexible and privileged shape in medicinal chemistry and is broadly used as a template for drug designing and drug discovery, which can be because of the handy synthesis method [13]. Several reviews highlighting the importance of chalcones as antimicrobial and antiparasitic retailers had been documented withinside the literature [14]. Chalcones (Fig. 1.1) had been used as intermediates for the instruction of compounds with healing value. A wide variety of artificial routes had been pronounced for the synthesis of chalcones, the Claisen-Schmidt condensation has homogeneous situations in the presence of acid or base is the maximum used.

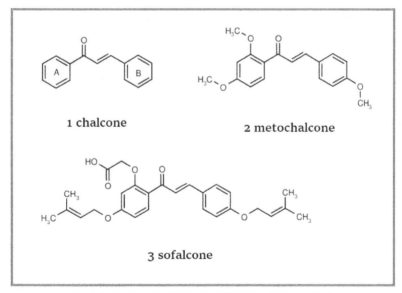

1 chalcone

2 metochalcone

3 sofalcone

FIG.1.1 GENERAL STRUCTURES OF CHALCONE

Naturally happening chalcones derived from widespread meals are phloretin and its glucoside, phloridzin, chalconaringenin, and arbutin [15]. Most of the research to date, concerning tactics of chalcone derivatives, has been pronounced through the natural and medicinal chemists via the formation of the 1,4-enones the usage of acid or base-catalyzed condensation reactions of aldehyde and aryl methyl ketones in alcoholic solvents with variable yields [16]. Natural chalcones arise as petal pigments and feature additionally been determined in the fireside wood, bark, leaf, fruit, and root of a whole lot of bushes and plant life [17]. They are some of the maximum applicable plant pigments for flower coloration, generating yellow or red and blue pigmentation in petals, designed to draw pollinator animals like bees. In better plant life they may be additionally worried about UV filtration [18], symbiotic nitrogen fixation [19], and floral pigmentation [20]. Chalcones arise clearly in plant life along with Angelica keiskei [21], Glycyrrhiza inflates [22], and Piper aduncum [23] and feature lengthy been used as medicinal plant life in Asia, Africa, and South America [24], that have been utilized in conventional medication to deal with sicknesses along with most cancers and antibacterial or parasitic infections. Polyhydroxylated chalcones are commonly available in nature and finds their applications due to the presence of phenolic chemical group. The usage of the compounds or chalcone wealthy plant extracts as pills or meal preservatives [25].

Chalcones are a collection of plant-derived polyphenolic compounds belonging to the flavonoids own circle of relatives that own a huge form of cytoprotective and modulatory functions, which might also additionally have healing capacity for more than one sickness [26]. Their physicochemical residences appear to outline the quantity in their organic activity. A complete of the latest patent literature (2005-2011) describing chalcones and their derivatives on decided on sports [27]. Natural merchandise are referred to as wealthy resets of bioactive molecules and chemical range and feature therefore furnished valuable chemical scaffolds, in addition, to serving as a concept closer to antibacterial drug discovery and improvement [28].

The numerous herbals and artificial chalcones and their derivatives seem like promising anti-inflammatory and anti-most cancers [29]. Their medical assessment may be important to evaluate their healing utility. Those for which the mechanism of movement is nicely described can function as lead compounds for the layout of the latest promising molecules. Chalcones own conjugated double bonds and a totally delocalized p-electron machine on each benzene rings[30]. Due to the enone system, such molecules gift quite low redox potentials and feature opportunity for present process electron switch reactions. Chalcones belong to the most important magnificence of plant secondary metabolites and are taken into consideration to be precursors of flavonoids and isoflavonoids serving in plant protection mechanisms to counteract reactive oxygen species to continue to existprevent molecular damage and damage by microorganisms, insects, and animals.

The chalcone is pronounced as an herbal precursor of an isoflavonoid, in fact, it's far an unsaturated fragrant ketone along with two phenyl rings, related through an enone moiety [31]. The cyclization of chalcones result in the formation of the isoflavonoid and flavone shape [32]. Chalcones can exist in isomeric paperwork (Z) and (E), of which the (E)-isomer is considered thermodynamically favourable [33]. Chalcones are powerful steel ion chelators, and they can without difficulty create steel-coordinated compounds [34]. All kinds of chalcones own three fundamental domain names to engage with metals for instance the 3,4-dihydroxy machine placed in polyhydroxy chalcones, the ketone moiety, and the olefinic moiety. Various adjustments of the substituents on the phenyl rings are possible, by changing the phenolic -OH institution into -OR,-OC(O)R, or -OC(O)OR functionalities. Further functionalization may be achieved, for instance, through alkylation on the α,β-unsaturated carbonyl moiety in a Michael addition response [35].

They synthesized a sequence of herbal chromophoric merchandise in the 19th century. The chalcone scaffold serves because the precursor of flavonoids and isoflavonoids and is the open chain intermediate in the aurone synthesis. Chalcones and flavanones are isomeric and go through inter-conversion with ease in the presence of acid or base, wherein the former acts as a catalyst for chalcone formation and the latter aids in flavanones formation [36]. The chemistry of chalcones remained a fascination amongst researchers in the twenty-first century because of its easy chemistry, ease of synthesis, and a massive wide variety of replaceable hydrogens to yield a massive wide variety of derivatives. Chalcone scaffold in conjugation with the different heterocyclic nuclei, specifically pyrazole, pyrimidine, isoxazole, pyrazoline, thiadiazole, benzoxazepine, benzodiazepine, benzothiazepine serves as promising for synthesizing pharmacologically active compounds. Traditionally, the scaffold is fabricated through the Claisen-Schmidt response wherein an equimolar amount of benzaldehyde and acetophenone are reacted in the presence of 40 percent of sodium hydroxide solution. In addition to it, several call reactions along with Suzuki-Miyaura response, Friedel-Crafts response, Julia-Kocienski response, Sonogashira isomerization coupling, Carbonylated Heck coupling response, Direct crossed coupling response are pronounced to offer an excessive yield of the compounds [37]. Other inexperienced artificial techniques like solvent unfastened synthesis, one-pot synthesis, microwave-assisted synthesis, and strong acid catalyst mediated synthesis are likewise hired for the fabrication of the benzylidene acetophenone scaffold. The inhibitory views of the scaffold consist of important inhibition of the enzymes, channels, and receptors worried in hyperactive states in any biomolecular direction and play a vital function in the exaggeration of the sicknesses.

In this context, synthesis and assessment of herbal product-stimulated compounds libraries to constitute an appealing technique for coming across novel antibacterial retailers [38]. Chalcones are vital precursors in the biosynthesis of flavones and flavanones and are normally synthesized from acetophenones and benzaldehydes through the Claisen-Schmidt condensation, the usage of a base in a polar solvent [39]. In addition, greater wonderful artificial protocols had been pronounced, along with the palladium mediated Suzuki coupling among cinnamoyl chloride and phenylboronic acids or the carbonylative Heck coupling with aryl halides and styrene in the presence of carbon monoxide [40]. The chromenone ring of 1-benzopyran-4-one is the center fragment in numerous flavonoids, along with flavones, flavanols and isoflavones. The inflexible bicyclic chromenone fragment has been categorized as a privileged shape in drug discovery because of its use in a huge form of pharmacologically lively compounds [41]. Several chromenone derivatives have additionally been pronounced to behave as kinase inhibitors, bind to benzodiazepine receptors, and as green retailers in the remedy of cystic fibrosis. Although there is wide variety of chromenone derivatives recognized for their pharmacological properties there are just a few examples that have been can be used as healing retailers today [42]. The unusual place artificial routes to the chromenone shape arise through a chalcone intermediate [43]. The chalcone pathway implicates the base-catalyzed aldol condensation of 2′-hydroxy acetophenones with fragrant or conjugated aldehydes [44]. The ensuing chalcone can then be cyclized to a flavone or the corresponding 3-hydroxyflavone, the usage of alkaline hydrogen peroxide solution, through the Algar-Flynn Oyamada (AFO) response. The chromenone shape can then be acquired through acid- catalyzed cyclization [45]. Several opportunity routes to reap chromenones and flavones had been pronounced over the current years, along with the cyclization of alkynyl-ketones or palladium-mediated cyclo carbonylation of ortho-iodophenol with terminal acetylenes in the presence of carbon monoxide.

Various organic activities had been attributed to chalcones, together with antimicrobial, antibiotic, antiparasitic, antimalarial, anti-inflammatory, analgesic, and anesthetic properties [46]. Several chalcones had been credited for medical use, together with the choleretics meto chalcone and the antiseptic ulcer much shielding sofalcone.

5

1.2 EXPERIMENTAL
DIFFERENT SYNTHETIC METHODS FOR CHALCONE SYNTHESIS

1. Claisen-Schmidt Reaction

2. Suzuki Coupling Reaction

3. Direct Cross-coupling Reaction

4. Coupling Reaction

5. Witting Reaction

SYNTHETIC METHOD OF PREPARING CHALCONES

The most convenient method is the Claisen-Schmidt condensation of equimolar quantities of aryl methyl ketone with aryl aldehyde in the presence of alcoholic alkali [47].

CLAISEN-SCHMIDT REACTION

A variety of methods are available for the synthesis of chalcones, the most convenient method is the one that involves the Claisen-Schmidt condensation (Fig. 1.2) of equimolar quantities of substituted acetophenone with substituted aldehydes in the presence of aqueous alcoholic alkali [48]. In the Claisen-Schmidt reaction, the concentration of alkali used usually ranges between 10 and 60 % [49]. The reaction is carried out at about 50°C for 12-15h or at room temperature for one week. Under these conditions, the Cannizaro reaction [50], also takes place and thereby decreases the yield of the desired product. To avoid the disproportionation of aldehyde in the above reaction, the use of benzylidene-diacetate in place of aldehyde has been recommended [51].

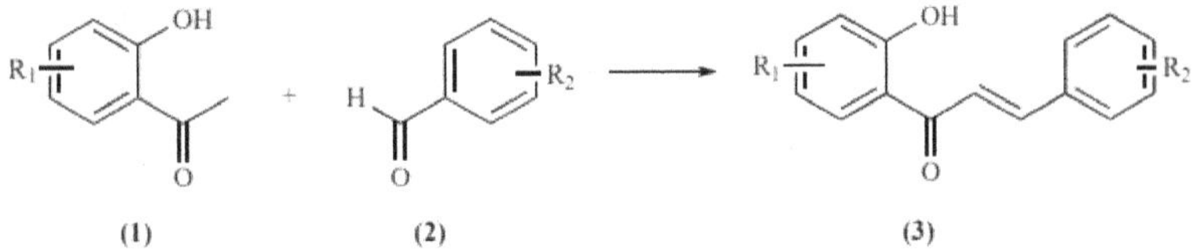

(1)   (2)   (3)

FIG. 1.2 CLAISEN-SCHMIDT REACTION

This reaction has been found to work without any solvent at all a solid-state reaction. In a study investigating green chemistry synthesis, chalcones were also synthesized from the same starting materials in high-temperature water (200 to 350 °C). Alternatively, the substituted chalcones were synthesized by piperidine-mediated condensation to avoid side reactions such as multiple condensations, polymerizations, and rearrangements. Diffraction techniques are the maximum powerful approach to analyzing solids in popular. In the look at substances for strength storage devices (batteries, and many others), they are notably used in the improvement and management of electrode substances.

1.3 GEOMETRICAL PARAMETER ESTIMATES

1.3.1 BOND LENGTH

3D Crystal structure determination provides valuable information regarding the crystallographic parameters and atomic coordinates. In a crystal system if two atoms are given by the position (x_1, y_1, z_1) and (x_2, y_2, z_2), then in the structure their inter atomic distances can be estimated using standard formula, which helps to describe the bond order (Fig. 1.3).

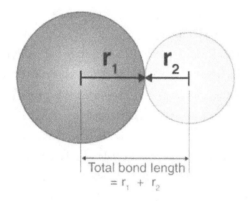

FIG. 1.3 BOND LENGTH

1.3.2 BOND ANGLE

A-B-C, is the perspective among the bond A-B and B-C shaped via 3 atoms A, B, and C, related in that order (Fig.1.4). If the period of A-B= I_1, B-C = I_2, and AC= I_3, then the perspective A-B-C can be calculated as

$$Cos\ \delta = (I_1^2 + I_2^2 - I_3^2) / (2I_1I_2)$$

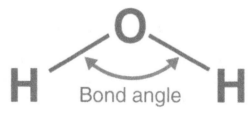

FIG. 1.4 BOND ANGLE

7

Apart from giving the info on the molecular shape, bond angles also are beneficial to looking at the hybridization of the atoms

1.3.3 TORSION ANGLE

In a nonlinear chain of atoms, A-B-C-D, the perspective among the planes is containing atoms ABC and the aircraft containing BCD. The torsion perspective will have any value from 0 to 180°. If the chain is considered alongside the BC, the torsion angle is positive if the bond AB could be turned around in a (Fig.1.5) clockwise sense (much less than 180°) to eclipse (i.e, align with) the bond CD. If the rotation of A must be in an anticlockwise sense, the torsion perspective could be negative.

$$\theta = \cos^{-1}\left[\frac{\overrightarrow{N1}.\overrightarrow{N2}}{|\overrightarrow{N1}||\overrightarrow{N2}|}\right]$$

where, $\overrightarrow{N_1}$ and $\overrightarrow{N_2}$ and the normal to the ABC and BCD planes, respectively.

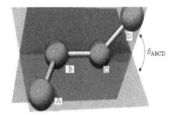

FIG. 1.5 TORSION ANGLE

1.3.4 INTER AND INTRA MOLECULAR INTERACTIONS

In a crystalline state, the molecules are stabilized by the non-covalent interactions (NCI) between the atoms of the molecule. The interaction between two negatively charged atoms play a vital role in stabilizing the structure, in which the hydrogen atom is covalently bonded to donor and acceptor atoms. The traditional manner of representing the hydrogen bond is D-H...A, and the D-H...A perspective needs to be 180°. The sum of the van der Waals radii of donor and acceptor atom should be slightly lesser or equal to the distance between them. Atoms and molecules with no net charges are held together by the weakest molecular forces. Therefore, there are no resultant attractive or repulsive forces remains other than less residual forces.

1.3.5 CONFORMATION OF RINGS

Conformation of any ring system is nothing but the shape assumed by it due to the chemical environment and chemical group substitutions. Conformational difference observed in the five, six, eight & ten membered ring systems is due to the chemical environment in the crystal structure and the disturbing forces between the chemical groups of the molecule result from the truth that every atom inside a molecule occupies a certain amount of space. At the closest distance, the atoms may lose some quantum of energy due to superposition of electron gas (Pauli or Born repulsion), and this may affect the molecules preferred shape (conformation) and reactivity. The exclusive conformations adopted via the rings can be confirmed by the mirror plane perpendicular to the plane of a ring or a two-fold axis passing through the ring. There are six different conformations were assumed by six-membered rings (Fig.1.6), while five membered ring adopts on three conformations (Fig.1.7). Recently, the eight and ten membered rings (Figs. 1.8 & 1.9) were also observed to exhibit new class of conformations. In general the conformation assumed by any ring system is evaluated via puckering parameters by following the criterion framed by Cremer & Pole and also by asymmetry parameters by Nardelli. M. In the present work the Cremer & Pole criterion were used in total to analyze the conformations of the heterocyclic rings of all the five compounds.

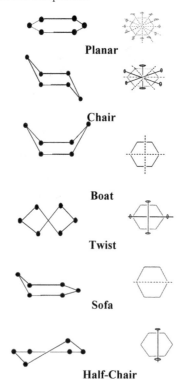

Planar

Chair

Boat

Twist

Sofa

Half-Chair

9

FIG. 1.6 PUCKERED CONFORMATION OF THE SIX-MEMBERED RINGS

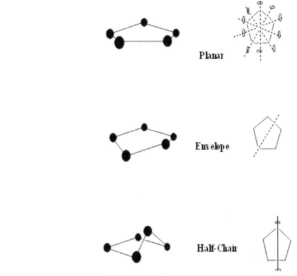

Planar

Envelope

Half-Chain

FIG. 1.7 PUCKERED CONFORMATION OF THE FIVE-MEMBERED RINGS

"Boat–Boat" (BB) Conformation   "Chair–Chair" (CC) Conformation   "Boat–Chair" (BC) Conformation
energetically preferred

FIG. 1.8 PUCKERED CONFORMATION OF THE EIGHT-MEMBERED RINGS

"Chair–Chair–Chair" (CCC) Conformation   "Boat–Chair–Boat" (BCB) Conformation
energetically preferred

FIG. 1.9 PUCKERED CONFORMATION OF THE TEN-MEMBERED RINGS

1.3.6 COMPUTATION IN CRYSTALLOGRAPHY

Computational applications play a curial position in the shape dedication of crystals via way of means of X-ray crystallographic technique. Those are indexed in the following steps, the depth records series, Lorentz, and polarization correction have been accomplished the use of the APEX2 software program. The WinGX suite offers an entire set of applications for the small molecular single crystal diffraction records, from records discount and processing, shape solution, version refinement and visualization, and metric evaluation of molecular geometry and crystal packing, to very last file to final report preparation in the form of a CIF. The application for windows offers a Graphical User Interface (GUI) for the conventional ORTEP application, that the authentic software program for the instance of anisotropic displacement ellipsoids. The applications WinGX and ORTEP for home windows had been allotted over the net for approximately 15 years, and this newsletter describes the several greater cutting-edge capabilities of the applications. WinGX [52] is the wholesome crystallographic software program used to solve the crystal structure and analyze the crystallographic information [53], the WinGX suite comprised a few trendy applications, together with SHELX-97 [54], Mercury [55], PARTS [56], and ORTEP-3 [57], SHELX-97 is the maximum upgraded model of the laptop bundle for the crystal shape dedication from single crystal diffraction records. The CIF [58] is designed for the digital transmission of crystallographic records among person laboratories, journals, and databases, it's been followed via the International Union of Crystallography because the advocated medium for this purpose. The document includes records names and records items, collectively with a loop facility for repeated items. The winGX software is the platform incorporating the subprograms called PARST and ORTEP to elucidate the crystal parameters and to display the molecular structure of the compounds. PLATON [59] is an important aid to estimates crystal parameters. International union of crystallography (IUCr) is rendering parallel less service to the field of crystallography in terms of assessing the chemical compounds for their correct structure and analysis, maintaining crystallographic data bank and publishing research papers on various crystal aspects.

1.3.7 CRYSTAL PACKING FEATURES

Molecular solids as the "understanding of intermolecular interactions in the context of crystal packing and the utilization of such understanding in the design of new solids with desired physical and chemical properties [60]. Crystal packing combines color mapping on molecular surfaces of properties derived from molecular wave functions and the efficient calculation of remarkably reliable intermolecular interaction energies [61] along with a graphical representation of their magnitude [62]. The interactions between atoms can be strong. Comparatively strong interactions are conventionally called ordinary chemical bonds. The covalent or ionic or metallic bonds are of this kind, and they form one of the most fundamental concepts of chemistry. Less strong interactions, say with bond energies significantly below 100 kJ/mol, are called weak or secondary interactions van der Waals, the polarization, the dispersion interactions, hydrogen bonds, metallophilic bonds, and so on [63]. The molecular interactions play a crucial position in chemistry, especially in cutting-edge chemistry together with supramolecular chemistry, crystal engineering, surface science, and bio disciplines. The investigation of weak interaction has attracted a great deal of interest in recent years [64]. The weak interaction may be intra-molecular or inter-molecular. The intra-molecular weak interaction is very crucial to apprehend the conformations of molecules and deviations from trendy systems. Two examples for this subject matter are a) Intramolecular hydrogen bonds in natural, inorganic, organic, and organ metallic compounds [65]. b) Steric interplay.

1.4 HIRSHFELD SURFACES AND ENERGY FRAMEWORKS RESEARCH

1.4.1 HIRSHFELD SURFACES

The Hirshfeld surfaces, two-dimensional fingerprint plots, and the color-coded interaction energies mapping have been generated to apprehend and quantify the weak inter molecular interactions using software program Crystal Explorer 17.5 [66]. In the latest past, the evaluation of calculated Hirshfeld surfaces has to turn out to be an indispensable tool for crystallographers and crystal designers, as these statistics concerning the position of weak intermolecular interactions in the packing of molecules in crystals. These are surfacing in which the ratios between the density weights function of the pro-molecule and the pro-crystal are 0.5a.u. (isosurface). Unlike van der Waals surface, these surfaces recall the closest neighboring molecules, and consequently offer information about intermolecular interactions [67, 68]. Compartmentalization of the generated surface through d_i and d_e values in a pair (d_i, d_e) and becoming into the periods of 0.2 Å results in the generation of 2D fingerprint plots. In addition, those (d_i, d_e) pairs while normalized for the van der Waals radii in their respective atoms effects in the d_{norm} surface. The red color on the d_{norm} surface represents contacts shorter than the sum of the van der Waals radii of the two atoms resulting in a negative value. Contacts with lengths approximate to the van der Waals restriction are colour white, and blue color illustrates longer contacts. The Hirshfeld surfaces mapped over the molecular electrostatic potential can be generated using the computational software package Tonto [69], integrated into the Crystal Explorer 17.5 application, which authorizes the visualization of the donors and acceptors of intermolecular interactions through blue and red areas around the participating atoms corresponding to positive and negative electrostatic potential on the surface, respectively.

The shape-index is an approximate quantification of the geometrical shape (triangle), which is sensitive even to minute modifications in surface shape (flat region), while Hirshfeld surface mapped at the surface assets curvedness is the degree of the flatness of the are especially ring structures, with the excessive curvedness is highlighted as dark-blue boundaries. These two surfaces analysis were introduced by Koendrink [70-72], offer extra statistics concerning the molecular packing in the crystal. The presences of adjoining blue and red triangles in the ring structures over shape-index, and curvedness is illustrating the existence of $\pi...\pi$ stacking interactions. Also, shape-index > 1or < 1 represents the donor and acceptor atoms of intermolecular interaction, respectively. Hirshfeld surface which incorporates d_e and d_i in pair may be applied to generate 2D fingerprint plots [73,74] representing the contribution because of diverse interatomic interactions. The color of every phase at the surface relative to the region of a (d_e, d_i) pair is recounted because of the complement from exclusive interatomic contacts. The frequency of incidence of the interatomic interactions varies as blue, and red, which illustrate the potential contribution to the full Hirshfeld surface modifications as lowest-mild largest. The delineated 2D fingerprint plots received from the full 2D fingerprint plot may be a powerful representation to derive the complicated molecular interaction info hidden in a crystal.

1.4.2 ENERGY FRAMEWORKS

A new computational and graphical device to calculate pairwise intermolecular interaction energies for natural and a few inorganic molecular crystals, whose employment in fabricating 'energy frameworks' offers an indomitable however new manner to visualize the supramolecular structure of molecular crystal systems [75], however with boundaries energy frameworks have been restrained to electrostatic and dispersion energy terms, similarly, total energies of the negative sign by assuming that those are the stabilizing energies the crystal systems of impartial molecules. Fundamentally, ionic crystals integrate large positive destabilizing (cation-cation and anion-anion), as well as large negative(cation-anion) energies and those want to be represented as a part of an energy-framework picture. To consist of those destabilizing energies, the implementation of energy frameworks [75] now includes extra cylinders of various colorations to energy framework diagrams red for the electrostatic term, green for dispersion, and blue is total energy. The pair-wise interaction energies within a crystal may be obtained by adding four energy additives namely, electrostatic (E_{ele}), polarization (E_{pol}), dispersion (E_{dis}), and change-repulsion (E_{rep}), and by fitting into the expression, viz $E_{\text{total energy}} = E_{\text{electrostatic energy}} + E_{\text{Polarization energy}} + E_{\text{dispersion energy}} + E_{\text{repulsion energy}}$, based on the energy model called counterpoise-corrected B3LYP-D2/6-31G (d,p). The calculation of interaction energies for crystal systems is commonly easy, where in users want to generate a cluster of molecules inside a radius of 3.8 Å for a particular reference molecule and sooner or later issue it to energy calculation upon placing the applicable parameters together with molecular charge, multiplicity, and energy version. The calculation of molecular interaction energies not only provides information about the four energy components but also details about the existence of rotational symmetry operations, the centroid-to-centroid distance among the reference molecule and interacting molecules, and the wide variety of pairs of interacting molecules with admire to the reference molecule. Visualization of those energies and their electrostatic and dispersion additives, in the shape of energy frameworks sheds light on the architecture of molecular crystals comprising metal coordination compounds, organic salts, solvates, and open-shell molecules.

1.5 BIOLOGICAL ACTIVITY STUDIES
1.5.1 ANTIMICROBIAL ACTIVITY

The first antimicrobial agent in the world was salvarsan, a treatment for syphilis that was synthesized by Ehrlich in 1910 [76]. In 1935, sulphonamides had been developed by Domagk and different researchers. These drugs had been synthetic compounds and had limitations in terms of safety and efficacy. The general traces of Gram-positive microorganism: *Salmonella typhi* and *Micrococcus luteu*, Gram-negative microorganism species: *Staphylococcus aureus* and *Pseudomonas aeruginosa,* and fungi species: *Candida albicans, Aspergillus niger, Trichoderma viride*, have been used in the present study. Stock solutions of the test compounds and general drug have been diluted two-fold in the microplate wells. Solutions of the synthesized compounds have been organized at 500,750, and 1000μg/mL concentrations and the drug (antibiotic) were organized at 1mg/mL concentration. During antibacterial susceptibility testing, 100 μL of Mueller Hinton Broth (MHB) was added to each well of the microplate, and the bacterial suspension of the bacteria at 10^5 CFU/mL concentrations was inoculated into the solutions of the compound. A 20 μL bacterial inoculum was added to each well of the microplates and is incubated at 37°C for 24 h. Then the antimicrobial activity was determined by measuring the diameter of the zone of inhibition [77]. Antifungal activity of the Sample was determined by disc diffusion method on Sabouraud Dextrose agar (SDA) medium [78]. SDA medium is poured into the Petri plate and after the medium was solidified, the inoculums were spread on the solid plates with a sterile swab moistened with the fungal suspension. Amphotericin-B is taken as a positive control. Samples and positive control of 20 μL each were added to sterile discs and placed in SDA plates. The plates were incubated at 28°C for 24h. Then the antifungal activity was determined by measuring the diameter of the zone of inhibition.

1.5.2 ANTIOXIDANT ACTIVITY

Antioxidants are components that can prevent harm to cells brought on through free radicals, unstable molecules that the body produces as a response to environmental and different pressures. They are on occasion referred to as "free-radical scavengers". The sources of antioxidants can be herbal or artificial. The antiradical activity of the compound changed into decided the usage of the free radical, 1,1-Diphenyl-1-picrylhydrazyl (DPPH). In its radical form, DPPH has an absorption band at 520 nm which disappears upon discount through an antiradical compound. Test tubes with 3.7 mL of absolute methanol in 100μL of the pattern and 200μL of DPPH solution at room temperature stirred for the 20s and have been left in the dark [79]. The absorbance of the solution at 517 nm changed into measured by the usage of a UV Spectrophotometer for which a blended solution of 100μL of absolute methanol and 100μL of Butylated Hydroxy Toluene (BHT) changed into used because of the blank. The absorbance measured with the pattern changed into expressed as, the absorbance on the addition of methanol changing the sample as absorbance on the blank, and the (%) of antioxidant activity into expected he usage of the relation

$$\text{Antioxidant activity in \%} = \frac{(\text{Absorbance at blank}) - (\text{Absorbance at test})}{(\text{Absorbance at blank})} \times 100$$

1.5.3 CYTOTOXICITY AND ANTICANCER ACTIVITY RESEARCH – MTT ASSAY

VERO cell lines (normal)and MCF-7 cell lines (cancerous) were obtained from the National Centre for Cell Sciences, Pune (NCCS). The cells were maintained in Gibco Dulbecco's Modified Eagle Medium (DMEM) supplemented with 10% FBS, penicillin (100 U/mL), and streptomycin (100 μg/mL) in a humidified atmosphere of 50 μg/mL CO_2 at 37°C. Cells $(1 \times 10^5/\text{well})$ were plated in 24-well plates and incubated at 37°C with a 5% CO_2 condition. After the cell reaches the confluence, the various concentrations of the sample were added and incubated for 24h. After incubation, the sample was removed from the well and washed with phosphate-buffered saline (pH 7.4) or DMEM without serum.100μL/well (5mg/mL) of 0.5% 3-(4,5-dimethyl-2-thiazolyl)-2,5-diphenyl-tetrazolium bromide (MTT) was added and incubated for 4h. After incubation, 1mL of DMSO was added to all the wells. The absorbance at 570nm was measured with a UV- Spectrophotometer using DMSO as the blank. Measurements were performed and the concentration required for a 50% inhibition (IC_{50}) was determined graphically. The anticancer activity test of the synthesized chalcone analog on MCF-7 breast carcinoma was also performed by MTT assay [80].

1.6 MOLECULAR DOCKING INVESTIGATION

Molecular docking is a key technique in structural molecular biology and computer assisted drug layout [81]. Ligand-protein docking intends to predict the predominant binding modes of a ligand with a protein of regarded three dimensional structures. Successful docking method search high dimensional areas efficiently and uses a scoring characteristic that effective ranks candidate dockings. Docking can be used to function digital screening on large libraries of compounds, rank the results, and suggest structural hypotheses of how the ligand inhibits the target, which is beneficial in lead optimization. AutoDock is an automatic process for predicting the interaction of ligands with bio macromolecular targets, the use of the Lamarckian Genetic Algorithm in conjunction with the conventional genetic algorithms, and simulated annealing. The empirical loose energy scoring characteristic will offer reproducible docking effects for ligands with about 10 flexible bonds, similarly to, visualizing conformations, visualizing interactions among ligands and proteins, and visualizing the affinity potentials created via AutoGrid. In the prevailing work, the ligand (small molecule), and targets (protein) interactions have been studied using the AutoDock4.2.6 software program bundle [82], and the preparation of ligand and protein for the in-silico procedure and visualizing the interactions among them have been accomplished using PyMOL [83] a picture software program.

1.7 OPTICAL, THERMAL, AND MECHANICAL CHARACTERIZATION TECHNIQUES & ANALYSIS

1.7.1 NMR- INSTRUMENTATION TECHNIQUE

^{1}H NMR and ^{13}C NMR spectra were effectively utilized to identifying the correct molecular shape of a natural compounds and each has an identical working principle. The sample tube, control console, and the sweeping coils are the functional parts of NMR instrument. During NMR spectrum recording, the sample used to be dissolved in deuterated chloroform solvent and then positioned centered on two magnetic poles, at the identical time radio frequency irradiated the sample with a quick pulse of radiation, inflicting resonance [84]. NMR spectra of the synthesized compounds have been recorded in deuterated chloroform with TMS (Tetra Methyl Silane) as the internal standard. In the present study, the NMR spectra have been recorded on BRUKER AVANCE 400MHz (AV 400) NMR Spectrometer.

1.7.2 FOURIER TRANSFORM INFRARED SPECTROSCOPY(FT-IR)

Infrared spectroscopy is a non-destructive technique for substance evaluation and is used to learn about of interaction of matter with the electromagnetic field in the IR radiation region as a characteristic of photon frequency. It gives some detail about each vibration and rotation of the chemical bonding and molecular structures, which is used to analyze organic and inorganic materials. In general, FTIR spectrum for the unknown samples has been recorded in the mid-IR $(4000\text{-}400\,\text{cm}^{-1})$ spectral range and is most beneficial in organic chemistry because the preferential absorption of the chemical groups remains in this region. In the present work, FTIR spectra for the samples were recorded by using BRUKER spectrometer.

1.7.3 FT-RAMAN INSTRUMENTATION TECHNIQUE

A modern, compact Raman spectrometer consists of various basic components, such as a laser that serves as the excitation source to induce the Raman scattering. Typically, solid-state lasers are used in present-day Raman instruments with famous wavelengths of 532nm, 785nm, 830nm, and 1064nm. The shorter wavelength lasers have greater Raman scattering crosssection, so the ensuing signal is greater, alternatively, the incidence of fluorescence also increase at shorter wavelength. For this reason, many Raman systems function with the 785nm laser. The laser energy is transmitted to and gathered from the sample by fiber optics cables. A notch or edge filter is used to take away Rayleigh and anti-stokes scattering and the remaining stokes scattered light is passed on to a dispersion element, commonly a holographic grating. A CCD detector captures the light, ensuing in the Raman spectrum. Since Raman scattering yields a weak signal, it is most necessary that high-quality, optically well-matched components. FT-Raman spectra were recorded by using BRUKER RFS 27 spectrometer.

1.7.4 ULTRAVIOLET-VISIBLE SPECTROSCOPY

UV-Visible spectroscopy additionally refers to absorption spectroscopy that includes learn about the interaction between the matter and energy in the 200-400nm spectral range which provide information for identifying and determining the type of conjugation among bonds. Ultra-violet region is extending from190-400nm, which is subdivided into two sections: The near UV region (200-400nm). The far region 10-200nm, and the visible region is prevails from 400-800nm. On a Cary 100 UV-Vis spectrophotometer, UV, Vis, and NIR spectra were captured for the current study.

1.7.5 PHOTOLUMINESCENCE SPECTROSCOPY (PL)

A non-destructive method of examining a materials spontaneously occurring electronic structure is photoluminescence spectroscopy method primarily based on the release of energy from the materials. Fluorescence, the optical happenings is based on the energy of the stimulating radiation is maintained and the emission occurred from a singlet excited state with a lifetime of between 10^{-10} and 10^{-7}s, photons (UV, Visible, and IR) will be absorbed by the material in the form of light. 2. The process of phosphorescence, which is based on the energy of photons absorbed by matter and the emission, was produced by triplet excited states with energies between 10^{-5} and 10^3 life time via the relaxation processes.

1.7.6 THERMAL ANALYSIS (TG/ DTA)

A collection of methods known as "thermal analysis" are focused on the identification of changes in the chemical and physical characteristics of the materials under thermal conditions. Techniques are the most extensively used thermal methods. Thermo gravimetric analysis requires keeping track of sample mass while temperature ranges are changed. The TGA thermogram revealed the purity of samples and determined the mechanism of their transformations by plotting the change of sample against temperature inside a specific range of temperature. It additionally provides many different thermal properties likes, decomposition kinetics, and analytical materials with oxidative and thermal stability. When conducting a differentiating thermal analysis, both the sample and the reference material are concurrently heated and their temperature differences are measured. The DTA thermogram displays temperature transitions (exothermic or endothermic shifts) by plotting the differential temperature against time or temperature the samples.

1.7.7 MECHANICAL STRENGTH-MICROHARDNESS STUDIES

Micro indentation hardness testing also known as microhardness testing, is extensively used to learn about fine-scale modifications in hardness, both intentional and accidental. The general definition that can be given is that hardness is a measure of the resistance to deformation of the materials. An important use of microhardness testing is to an indirect estimate of different mechanical characteristics of materials having a unique correction with their hardness. It performs a key function in device fabrication etc. Heat treaters have utilized the method for many years to consider the success of surface hardening remedies or to discover and assess decarburization. Metallographers and failure analysts use the approach for a host of purposes consisting of evaluation of homogeneity, and characterization of welding as an aid to phase identification. Although the term microhardness is commonly understood by its users, the word implies that the hardness is extraordinarily low, which is not the case. The applied load and the ensuing indent measurement are small relative to bulk tests, however the same hardness number is obtained. The usual approach to gain a hardness value is to measure the depth of an indentation left through an indenter of a unique shape, with a specific force applied for a precise time. There are three principal standard test methods for expressing the relationship between hardness and the size of the impression, these being used for Vickers for practical and calibration reasons, for this method is divided into a range of scales, described through a mixture of applied load and indenter geometry.

CHAPTER-II

3D CRYSTAL STRUCTURE DETERMINATION AND ANALYSIS

2. INTRODUCTION

X-ray crystallography has emerged as an important source of unambiguous data on the crystal and molecular structure of compounds. 3D structure evaluation by using X-ray diffraction methods is the special technique of determining the whole 3D illustration of the atoms in a crystal which is required to understand the nature of the chemical bonds, the features of molecules in organic contexts, and additionally to recognize the mechanics and dynamics of reactions. X-ray crystallography is a preferred method for solving crystal structures, in which a beam of X-rays whose wavelengths correspond to interatomic distances, strike a crystal and diffracts into many precise directions. From the angles and intensities of these diffracted beams, a crystallographer can produce a three-dimensional picture of the density of electrons inside the crystal. From this electron density, the average position of the atoms in the crystal, their chemical bonds, and disorder can be determined. The technique also revealed the shape and features of many organic molecules along with vitamins, drugs, proteins, and nucleic acids such as DNA. X-ray crystallography is still the chief method for characterizing the atomic structure of new materials and discerning materials that appear to other experiments. X-ray crystals structures can also account for unusual electronic or elastic properties of a material, shed light on chemical interactions and processes, or serve as the basis for designing pharmaceuticals against diseases. Modern X-ray crystallography provides the most powerful and accurate method for determining single crystal structures. This section provides an overview of the procedures and methods for X-ray crystallographic structure analysis of small organic molecules.

The crystal structure is described by the ordered association of atoms, ions, or molecules in a crystalline material, in terms of the geometry of the association of particles in the unit cells which performs a crucial position in determining the physical properties of a material. The unit cell is defined as the smallest repeating unit having the entire symmetry of the crystal structure. The positions of particles inside the unit cell are described by the fractional coordinates (x_i, y_i, z_i) along the cell edges, measured from a reference point. It is only necessary to report the coordinates of the smallest asymmetric subset of particles. This group of particles may be chosen so that it occupies the smallest physical space, which means that not all particles need to be physically located inside the boundaries given by the lattice parameters. All other particles of the unit cell are generated by the symmetry operations that characterize the symmetry of the unit cell. The series of symmetry operations of the unit cell is expressed officially as the space group of the crystal structure.

3D structure of both small and macromolecules provides information on various aspects, such as protein classification, function prediction, interactions with other compounds, enzymatic mechanisms, structure-based drug development, posttranslational modifications, etc. 3D structure is a huge hint for understanding how the protein works and using that information for different purposes, control or modifying protein function, predict what molecules bind to that protein and understand various biological interactions, assisting drug discovery or even design our own.

2.1 BIOLOGICAL IMPORTANCE OF CHALCONE DERIVATIVES

Chalcone compounds have a common chemical scaffold of 1,3-diaryl-2-propen-1-one also known as chalconoid that exists as Trans and cis isomers with the Trans isomer being thermodynamically more stable [85]. The chalcone family has attracted much interest not only from the synthetic and biosynthetic perspectives but also due to its broad interesting biological activities [86]. Therapeutic applications of chalcones trace back thousands of years through the use of plants and herbs for the treatment of different medical disorders, such as cancer, inflammation, and diabetes [87]. Several chalcone-based compounds have been approved for clinical use [88, 89]. The chalcone derivative meto chalcone was once marketed as a choleretic drug, while sofalcone was previously used as an antiulcer and much protective drug [90]. Chalcones are one of the major classes of naturally occurring compounds and are highly exploited in the field of medicinal chemistry due to their remarkable pharmacological activities [91]. They are considered important secondary metabolites precursors of flavonoids and isoflavonoids in plants [92]. Synthetically, chalcones can go through a variety of chemical reactions and are found to be important intermediaries in the synthesis of pyrazoline, isoxazole, and an assortment of heterocyclic compounds [93]. Many synthetic routes have been reported for the synthesis of chalcones [94] but the most typical synthesis involves the Claisen-Schmidt condensation under homogeneous conditions in the presence of acid or base [95, 96]. Numerous reports highlighted the wide range of pharmacological activities of chalcones [97]. Thus, it is possible to find chalcone derivatives with many useful properties such as anticancer [98], antioxidants [99, 100], anti-inflammatory [101], adenosine receptor ligands [102], anti-malarial [103, 104], antimicrobial [105], anti-HIV [106, 107] or anti-protozoal [108] among others. It has been shown that the removal of the β-unsaturated carbonyl system could hinder their biological

20

activities as the removal of this functionality makes them inactive or decreases the activity [109]. Although a great number of chalcones have been published in the literature, an overview of the recent scientific accounts describing the design of new molecules is still needed. This part of the thesis reports the synthesis processes and the results of the study of molecular structure, molecular interactions, binding affinity, and biological activity evaluation of the title molecules. Breast cancer (BC) is a recurring and fatal ailment noticed in females. Its repercussions on the human population are enormous including the major cause of cancer deaths. Next to skin cancer, breast cancer is the most common cancer diagnosed, accounting for 23% of the total cancer cases and 14% of the cancer deaths [110]. BC does not symbolize a single disease but rather some molecularly distinct tumors arising from the epithelial cells of the breast [111]. Breast cancer forms in the cells of the breasts and is the most common cancer diagnosed in women in the United States. BC can occur in both men and women, but it's far more common in women. Substantial support for breast cancer awareness and research funding has helped create advances in the diagnosis and treatment of breast cancer [112]. Breast cancer survival rates have increased, and the number of deaths associated with this disease is steadily declining, largely due to factors such as earlier detection, a new personalized approach to treatment, and a better understanding of the disease [113]. To predict and recommend the kind of treatment for cancer demands research at the molecular level and this involves cell lines, particularly, as in vitro models in cancer research. An MCF7 cell line is a commonly used breast cancer cell line that has been promoted for more than 40 years by multiple research groups [114]. It proves to be a suitable model cell line for breast cancer investigations worldwide, including those regarding anticancer drugs [115]. Mortality for a range of malignancies, including breast cancer, was among the highest in Europe [116], and "disgracefully" long waiting lists resulting in delayed diagnosis and treatment were thought to be at least partly responsible [117]. In 1998, in an attempt to address these inequalities and to improve outcomes for patients with breast cancer, the Department of Health issued a circular titled Breast cancer waiting for times-achieving the two-week target [118]. Worldwide, breast cancer comprises 10.4% of all cancer incidences among women, making it the second most common type of non-skin cancer (after lung cancer) and the fifth most common cause of cancer death. In 2004, breast cancer caused 519,000 deaths worldwide (7% of cancer deaths; almost 1% of all deaths) BC is about 100 times more common in women than in men, although males tend to have poorer outcomes due to delays in diagnosis [119]. Despite certain advances in cancer therapy, still there is considerable demand for developing efficient therapeutic agents to treat cancer.

21

Considering the wide spectrum of pharmacological properties of chalcones and their derivatives, an attempt has been made to synthesize and characterize a series of five new such derivatives as explained below

IUPAC Names of the synthesized compounds

1. (3E)-3-(2, 4-dimethoxyphenyl)methylidene)-2,3-dihydro-4H-1-benzopyran-4-one (DBDB)

2. (3E)-3-(4-methoxyphenyl)methylidene)- 2,3-dihydro-4H-1-benzopyran-4-one (MPDB)

3. (3E)-3-(2, 4, 5-trimethoxyphenyl)methylidene)- 2,3-dihydro-4H- 1-benzopyran-4-one (TPDB)

4. (3E)-3-(2, 3, 4-trimethoxyphenyl)methylidene)- 2,3-dihydro-4H- 1-benzopyran-4-one (TMDB)

5. (3E)-3-(2, 3-difluorophenyl)methylidene)- 2,3-dihydro-4H- 1-benzopyran-4-one (DFDB)

2.2 EXPERIMENTAL

2.2.1 Synthesis of (3E)-3-(2,4-dimethoxyphenyl) methylidene)-2,3-dihydro-4H-1-benzopyran-4-one (DBDB)

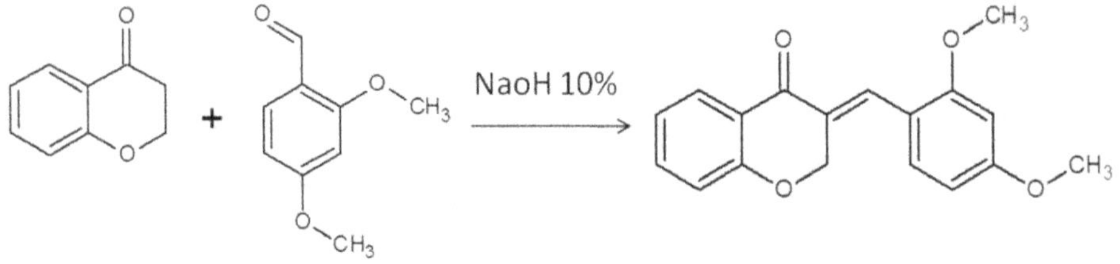

FIG. 2.1 REACTION SCHEME OF DBDB

The title compound, $C_{18}H_{16}O_4$, was synthesized by base catalyst Claisen-Schmidt condensation reaction. An aqueous solution of NaOH (10%, 10 mL) was added to a solution of 2,3-dihydro-4H-1-benzopyran-4-one and 2,4-dimethoxy benzaldehyde in 95% ethanol. The reaction mixture is stirred for 2h and is left overnight. A dark yellow colored solid is obtained after filtering and is washed with ice-cold water. The product is recrystallized by using ethanol

22

as solvent by the slow evaporation method. Yellow-colored transparent crystals of good quality are obtained after seven days. Fig.2.1. (Yield: 85%; MP: 133°C).

2.2.2 Synthesis of (3E)-3-(4-methoxyphenyl) methylidene)- 2,3-dihydro-4H-1-benzopyran-4-one (MPDB)

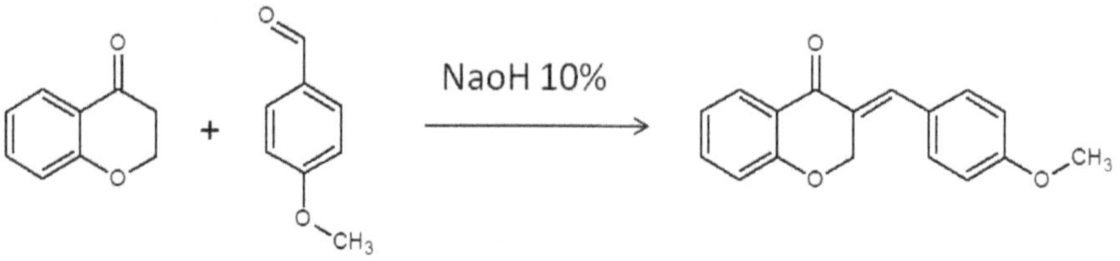

FIG. 2.1 REACTION SCHEME OF MPDB

A mixture of 2,3-dihydro-4H-1-benzopyran-4-one, and 4-methoxy benzaldehyde was prepared with 10% of NaOH and the mixtures were maintained well below 10°C. Ice cubes were added then to the mixture to improve the precipitation after 1h of stirring. The resultant precipitate was washed with distilled water for removing excess NaOH if any from the yield. Good quality single crystals of the title compound were grown in acetone and by the slow evaporation method. The chemical scheme representing the reaction is shown in Fig.2.1. (Yield: 95%; MP: 134°C).

2.2.3 Synthesis of (3E)-3-(2, 4, 5-trimethoxyphenyl) methylidene) - 2,3-dihydro-4H-1-benzopyran-4-one (TPDB)

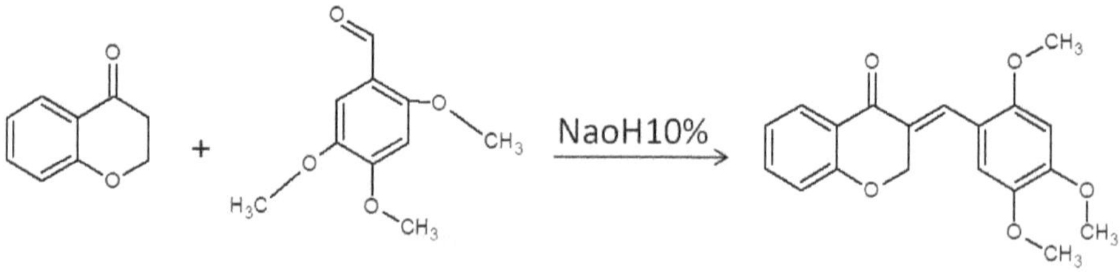

FIG. 2.1 REACTION SCHEME OF TPDB

The Mixture of 2,3-dihydro-4H-1-benzopyran-4-one and 2,4,5-trimethoxyphenyl methylidene was prepared with 10% of NaOH and maintained below 10°C temperature. Ice cubes were added to the mixture after 1h of stirring which enhances the precipitation capability. The precipitate was then collected and washed with distilled water for eliminating the excess NaOH from the resultant compound. Diffraction quality single crystals of the title derivative were grown using ethanol and by slow evaporation technique. The chemical scheme for the compound TPDB is shown in Fig. 2.1. (Yield: 85%; MP: 98°C).

2.2.4 Synthesis of (3E)-3-(2, 3, 4-trimethoxyphenyl) methylidene)-2,3-dihydro-4H-1-benzopyran-4-one (TMDB)

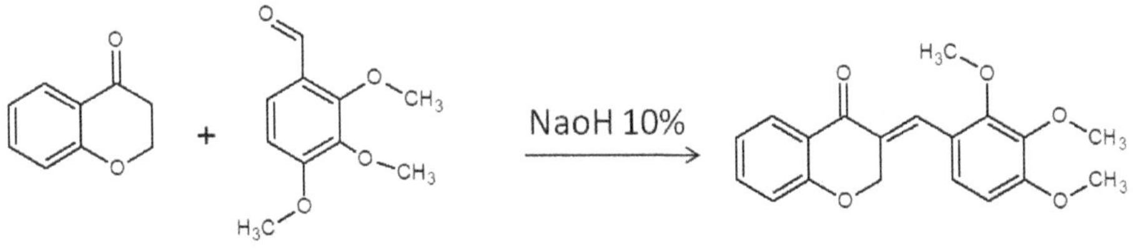

FIG. 2.1 REACTION SCHEME OF TMDB

2,3-dihydro-4H-1-benzopyran-4-one and 2,3,4 trimethoxy phenyl methylidene were dissolved in ethanol (50mL). The NaOH (10%) solution was added dropwise to the above solution and the temperature of the mixture was maintained below 10°C. The solution was stirred for about 3h and poured onto ice cubes. The yellow-colored precipitate was then collected and washed with distilled water to get the product free of NaOH. The product was recrystallized in ethanol and diffraction quality crystals were obtained by the slow evaporation method. The reaction scheme for the compound TMDB is shown in Fig.2.1. (Yield: 83%; MP: 128°C).

2.2.5 Synthesis of (3E)-3-(2, 3-difluoro phenyl) methylidene)-2, 3-dihydro-4H-1-benzopyran-4-one (DFDB)

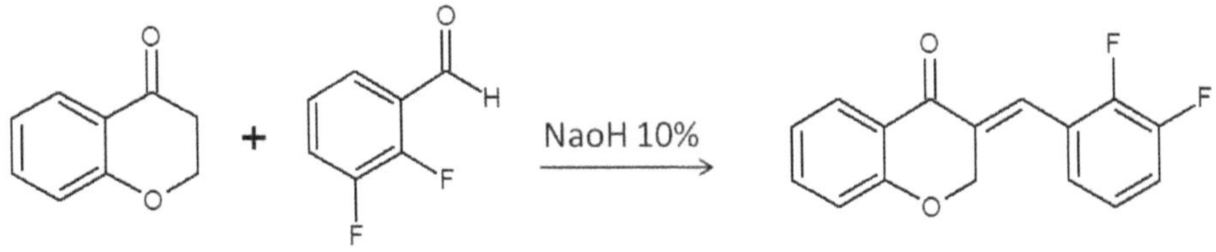

FIG. 2.1 REACTION SCHEME OF DFDB

The title compound, $C_{18}H_{16}O_4$, was synthesized by base catalyst Claisen-Schmidt condensation reaction. An aqueous solution of NaOH (10%, 10mL) was added to a solution of 2,3-dihydro-4H-1-benzopyran-4-one and 2,3-difluoro phenyl benzaldehyde in 95% ethanol. The reaction mixture is stirred for 2h and is left overnight. A dark yellow colored solid is obtained

24

after filtering and is washed with ice cold water. The product is recrystallized using ethanol as solvent by a slow evaporation method. Yellow-coloured transparent crystals of good quality are obtained after seven days Fig. 2.1. (Yield: 95%; MP: 129°C).

2.3 HIRSHFELD SURFACES AND ENERGY FRAMEWORKS INVESTIGATION

Hirshfeld surface (HS) analysis serves as a powerful tool for gaining additional insight into the intermolecular interactions of molecular crystals. The HS surrounding a molecule is defined in terms of the atomic electron densities of the "promolecule" and the "procrystal," and as such, for a molecule in a crystal, it is special and unlike other molecular surfaces. HS is created via an extension of the weight function describing an atom in a molecule to include the function of a molecule in a crystal. The isosurface generated from these calculations, with an exact weight function $w(r)=0.5$, surrounds the molecule and by partitioning the electron density of the molecular fragments, delineates the space occupied through a molecule in a crystal. HS can provide data about intermolecular interactions in the crystal as the surface is decided by each of the enclosed molecule and its closest neighbours. The size and shape of HS permit the wholesome exploration and visual display of short interactions available in the structures. The isosurface of two distances can be characterized: d_e, the distance from the point to the close by atom external to the surface, and d_i, the distance to the close by atom internal to the surface. Furthermore, the identification of the regions of particular significance to intermolecular interactions is obtained by mapping normalized contact distance (d_{norm}), expressed as:

$$d_{norm} = \frac{d_i - r_i^{vdW}}{r_i^{vdW}} + \frac{d_e - r_e^{vdW}}{r_e^{vdW}}$$

Another way to signify the HS is to generate an illustration that includes normalized contact distances thinking about the van der Waals radii of the atoms concerned in the analysis. This way of portraying the surface is named d_{norm}, this property is constituted through summation of the normalized contribution of d_e and d_i about the van der Waals radius of the atoms concerned in the expression. More concretely, this kind of analysis makes it possible to graphically illustrate the relative positioning of the neighboring atoms belonging to molecules interacting together. Again, a shade gradient is used to quantify the interactions taking region between the atoms inside the crystal being studied. This gradient varies from blue to green to red. By thinking about intermolecular interactions, the bluish domains point out that the distance keeping apart neighboring atoms exceeds the sum of their respective van der Waals radii. The white areas mark the locations where the distance separating the neighboring atoms is close to the sum of the van der Waals radii of the considered atoms. The red color on the d_{norm} surface represents contacts shorter than the sum of the van der Waals radii of the two atoms resulting in a negative value. From these facts, it is appropriate to expect the presence of non-covalent interactions between the atoms (or group of atoms) placed at the interface of the zones represented in red which exhibit a substantial approximation between these atoms. The HS and fingerprint plots are useful to understand the contributions of interatomic contacts and the stability of the molecular structure. The red color spot on the surface suggests the interatomic contacts involved in strong hydrogen bonding. The HS was recognized as the space occupied through a unit cell in a crystal system based on the electron distribution calculated around the spherical electron density in every atom. The HS is used to visualize inter molecular interactions with unique color codes. The acceptor systems are indicated by the red spots (hydrogen-bond acceptors) and the positive electrostatic potentials have been represented by a blue color (hydrogen-bond donors) [120].

Hirshfeld surfaces mapped over the surface properties such as d_{norm}, electrostatic potential, shape index, curvedness, and fragment patches, which authorizes visualization of the different types of interactions present within a crystal structure and the energy frameworks representing the network of nearest neighbor energies, was studied using Crystal Explorer 17.5 software [121]. The 2D fingerprint plots were also constructed and analyzed for the individual bonding contribution to the total Hirshfeld surface. Crystal Explorer 17.5 program, which authorizes the visualization of the donors and acceptors of intermolecular interactions via blue and red regions around the participating atoms corresponding to positive and negative electrostatic potential on the surface, respectively. In addition, Hartree-Fock/DFT (HF/DFT) theory-based wave-function calculations and surface generation can be affected using Tonto, a popular quantum chemistry package that may replace other packages like Gaussian16 [122].

2.4 RESULTS AND DISCUSSION
2.4.1 INTENSITY DATA COLLECTION

The diffraction quality crystals of size 0.200 x 0.200 x 0.150/ 0.200 x 0.200 x 0.150/ 0.200 x 0.200 x 0.180/ 0.300 x 0.250 x 0.200 and 0.200 x 0.200 x 0.150 mm were obtained by the slow evaporation. The crystal data were collected using a diffraction quality crystal on the goniometer head of the BRUKER AXS KAPPA APEX2-CCD diffractometer with MoKα (λ = 0.71073 Å) as an X-ray radiation source from Sophisticated Analytical Instruments Facility (SAIF), IITM, Chennai. The 3D crystal structure was solved and refined using the SHEL-XS 97

[123] and SHEL-XL/XT-18 [124] software, respectively, by employing a full matrix least-squares procedure on F^2. The Program PLATON [125] a multipurpose Crystallographic tool was utilized to calculate the crystal parameters such as bond lengths, bond angles, torsion angles, dihedral angles, intra and intermolecular interactions, and conformation of the ring systems.

2.4.2 STRUCTURAL ANALYSIS OF THE COMPOUNDS
DBDB

The intensity data collection and refinement details are given in Table 2.1.1. The isotropic and anisotropic displacement parameters of non-hydrogen atoms are listed in Tables 2.1.2 and 2.1.3, respectively. The hydrogen coordinates and least squares planes are listed in Table 2.1.4 and Table 2.1.7, respectively. In the title compound (Fig.2.2), experimentally estimated C-C and C=C bond distances of the phenyl ring C1-C6 and C11-C16 are in the range 1.368(1)-1.403(1) and 1.364(1)-1.403(1)(Å), respectively, and the other C-C single bond distances in the structure are lies between 1.450(1)-1.508(1) Å. The elongation observed in the C=C distances of the phenyl rings is attributed to the fusion between the rings about C5-C6 and the methoxy groups at C14 and C16. The C-O bond distances [1.364(1)-1.436(1)(Å)] and C=O distance of the chromenone ring is 1.220(1) Å (Table 2.1.5) and are in good agreement with similar reported structure [126,127]. The torsion angle C18-O4-C16-C11=175.97(1)° and C17-O3-C14-C15= 0.16(1)°, indicates that the methoxy group is in +anti-periplanar (+ap) and syn-periplanar (+sp) orientation, respectively, to the benzene ring (C11-C16). The torsion angle O2-C7-C8-C9=171.66(2)° and C9-O1-C6-C5=24.03(2)°, indicates that is in +anti-periplanar (+ap) and syn-periplanar (+sp) orientation, respectively, concerning the chromenone ring (Table 2.1.6). The dihedral angle between the mean aromatic planes is 57.42(1)°, which shows the bisectional orientation with each other (Table 2.1.8). The carbonyl oxygen O2 tends to be coplanar with the chromenone ring, which is revealed by the symmetry between the bond angles O2-C7-C5 [121.7(3)] and O2-C7-C8 [122.5(3)°]. In the title compound, the central cyclohexane ring [O1/C5-C9] adopts a distorted half chair conformation with ring puckering parameters; q2=0.3690(2) Å, phi2=77.4(3)°, q3=-0.1627(2) Å, QT=0.4033(2) Å and θ= 113.79(2)° [128]. The title compound, $C_{18}H_{16}O_4$, adopted

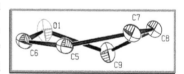

E-configuration for the double bonds C8=C10. The atomic coordinates of hydrogen atoms are listed in Table 2.1.4. The bond lengths and bond angles involving non-hydrogen atoms are presented in Table 2.1.5. Fig.2.2 shows the ORTEP plot of the title compound DBDB, drawn at

30% probability displacement ellipsoids along with atom labelling. The hydrogen bonds, non-hydrogen, and various contact contributions in the Hirshfeld surface are shown in Table 2.1.9-11 respectively,

Crystal Packing Features

In the crystal packing, the adjacent molecules are linked via C-H...O forming a chain with deep bending and they are interlocked in such a way that there appear to generate2D a network, but not so because the chains running along the 'a' axis are not linked by any inter molecular interaction. The packing of the molecules in the title compound viewed along the 'a' axis is shown in Fig. 2.3,and the unit cell packing for clarity drawn using Mercury software is also shown in Fig.2.3.

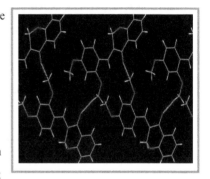

MPDB

The title compound crystallizes with two molecules in the asymmetric unit. The intensity data collection and refinement details are given in Table 2.2.1. The isotropic and anisotropic displacement parameters of non-hydrogen atoms are listed in Tables 2.2.2 and 2.2.3. The hydrogen coordinates and least squares planes are listed in Table 2.2.4 and Table 2.2.7. In the molecular structure, experimentally estimated C-C and C=C bond distances of the phenyl ring C1-C6 & C11-C16 and C18-C23,C28-C33 are in the range [1.375(3)-1.472(2) (Å)] & [1.372(2)-1.408(2) (Å)] and [1.369(1)-1.402(1) (Å)] & [1.377(1)-1.416(1) (Å)], respectively. The elongation observed in the C=C distances of the phenyl rings is attributed to the fusion between the rings about C5-C6 & C22-C23 and the methoxy groups at C14 and C31.The C-O bond distances [1.365(2)-1.432(1) (Å)] and C=O distance of the chromenone ring C7-O1 & C24-O4 are 1.225(2) & 1.234(1) Å (Table 2.2.5) and are in good agreement with the similar reported structures [126, 127]. The torsion angle O2-C15-C14-C13=-179.9(3)°and C4-C5-C6-O1= 0.5(1)°, indicates that the methoxy group is in -anti-periplanar (-ap) and syn-periplanar (+sp) orientation, respectively, to the benzene ring (Table 2.2.6). The dihedral angle between the mean aromatic planes is 59.67(2)°, which shows the bisectional orientation with each other (Table 2.2.8). The carbonyl oxygen O1 & O4 tend to be coplanar with the chromenone ring, which is revealed by the symmetry between the bond

angles O1-C7-C6 [121.9(1)°] and O1-C7-C8 [122.0(2)°] &
O4-C24-C23 [121.6(1)°] and O4-C24-C25 [121.9(1)°].In the
title compound, the central cyclohexane ring [O2/C5-C9] and

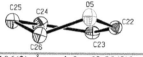

[O5/C22-C26] adopts a distorted half chair conformation with
ring puckering parameters$q2$=0.3687(2) Å, phi2=71.69(2)°, q3=
-0.1998(2) Å, QT= 0.4194(2) Å and   θ= 118.45(2)° and

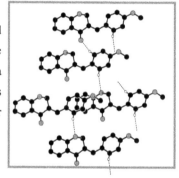

$q2$=0.3655(2) Å, phi2=-105.49(2)°, q3=0.1871(2) Å, QT= 0.4106(2) Å, and θ= 62.90(2)°
[128]. The Geometry of the hydrogen, non-hydrogen, and various contact contributions in the
Hirshfeld surface is shown in Table 2.2.9, Table 2.2.10, and Table 2.2.11.

Crystal Packing Features

The packing of the molecules in the title compound
viewed along the 'a' axis is shown in Fig. 2.3. There are
two molecules in the asymmetric unit connected via
C-H...O type hydrogen bonds and also linked to two of its
symmetry-related molecules forming a molecular cluster
without any further linking as shown in Fig. 2.3.

TPDB

The intensity data collection and structure refinement details are listed in Table 2.3.1.
The isotropic and anisotropic displacement parameters of non-hydrogen atoms are listed in
Tables 2.3.2 and 2.3.3, respectively. The hydrogen coordinates and least squares planes are listed
in Table 2.3.4 and Table 2.3.7, respectively. The ORTEP plot representing the molecular
structure drawn at a 30% probability level [Fig.2.2], packing of the molecules within the unit cell
viewed along the 'b' axis [Fig. 2.3]. The chalcone derivative, $C_{19}H_{18}O_5$, crystallizes in a
monoclinic crystal system with space group C2/c. Structural characterization was carried out by
single crystal X-ray diffraction method and the crystal parameters are a = 23.481(3),
b = 6.9442(10), c = 21.854(3) Å,V=3293.6(8) Å^3, Z=8, Density (ρ) = 1.316 Mg/m^3. In the title
compound, experimentally estimated C-C and C=C bond distances of the phenyl ring are in the
range [1.340(2)-1.484(2) (Å)] and [1.378(3)-1.402(2) (Å)] and the other C-C single bond
distances in the structure are lies between [1.399(2) -1.472(2) (Å) and 1.402(2)-1.502(2) (Å)], C-
O bond distances [1.361(1)-1.450(2) (Å)], and C=O distances of the chromenone ring is
[1.225(1) Å]. The selected bond lengths and bond angles are listed in Table 2.3.5, and are in
good agreement with the similar reported structures [126,127]. The torsion angle of C14-C15-

C16-O3= -179.1(1)° shows that the methoxy group is in –anti periplanar (-ap) orientation with the chalcone ring. The torsion angle of O4-C13-C14-C15-=179.3(1)° shows that the methoxy group is in +anti periplanar (+ap) orientation with the chalcone ring. The torsion angle O1-C7-C8-C9= -162.17 (1)° and C7-C8-C9-O2 = -48.11(2)°, indicating that is in -anti-periplanar (-ap) and -syn-clinal (-sc) orientation, respectively, for the chromenone ring. The carbonyl oxygen O1 tend to be coplanar with the chromenone ring, which is revealed by the symmetry between the bond angles O1-C7-C8 [122.8(3)°] and O1-C7-C6 [121.9(1)°]. The various torsion angles for the compound are listed in Table 2.3.6. The dihedral angle between the two phenyl mean planes is 62.6(2)° and it reveals the equatorial

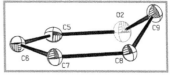

orientation between them [Table 2.3.8]. In the title compound, the central cyclohexane ring [O2/C6-C9] adopts a sofa conformation with ring puckering parameters are q2= 0.3647(2) Å, phi2 = -119.75(3)°, q3 = 0.2075(2)Å, QT = 0.4196(2) Å and Theta = 60.36(3)° [128]. The atomic coordinates of bonded, non-bonded, and various contact contributionson the Hirshfeld surface are given in Table 2.3.9-11, respectively.

Crystal Packing Features

In the compound, the molecular and crystal stability is due to the C-H...O hydrogen bonds. The molecule at (x, y, z) is linked to the symmetry-related molecules with equivalent position (1-x,-y,-z) via a pair of C-H...O intermolecular hydrogen bonds forming a dimer represented by the graph set motif R$_2^2$ (11) [129]. In the crystal packing, these dimers are arranged in a molecular sheet along the diagonal of the unit cell in the 'ac' plane. The packing of the molecules in the title compound viewed along 'b' axis is shown in Fig.2.3.

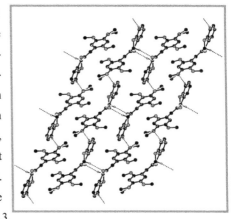

TMDB

The intensity data collection and structure refinement details are listed in Table 2.4.1. The isotropic and anisotropic displacement parameters of non-hydrogen atoms are listed in Tables 2.4.2 and 2.4.3, respectively. The hydrogen coordinates and least squares planes are listed in Table 2.4.4 and Table 2.4.7, respectively. The ORTEP plot representing the molecular structure drawn at a 30% probability level [Fig. 2.2], packing of the molecules within the unit cell viewed along the 'b' axis [Fig. 2.3]. In the title compound, experimentally estimated C-C and C=C bond distances of the phenyl ring C1-C6 and C11-C16 are in the range 1.368(2) -1.394(1) and 1.332(1) -1.405(1) (Å). The C-O bond distances [1.362(1)-1.439(1) (Å)] and C=O distance of the chromenone ring is 1.227(1) Å (Table 2.4.5), and those are in good agreement with similar reported structures [126, 127]. The torsion angle O4-C14-C13-C12 = 176.3(2)°, O2-C15-C14-C13 = -179.9(3)°, and O1-C16-C15-C14 =-176.4(1)° indicates that the methoxy groups are in +anti-periplanar (+ap),-anti-periplanar (-ap), and -anti-periplanar (-ap) orientation, respectively, to the benzene ring (C11-C16). The torsion angle C10-C8-C9-O5= 142.4(3)°, and O3-C7-C5-C4= -164.9(3)°, indicates that the atoms are in +anti-clinal (+ac) and -anti-periplanar (-ap) orientation, respectively, for the chromenone ring (Table 2.4.6). The dihedral angle between the mean aromatic planes is 55.30(1)°, which shows the bisectional orientation with each other (Table 2.4.8). The carbonyl oxygen O3 tends to be coplanar with the

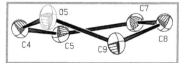

chromenone ring, which is revealed by the symmetry between the bond angles O3-C7-C8 [122.5(3)°] and O3-C7-C5 [121.9(3)°]. In the title compound, the central cyclohexane ring [O5/C4-C9] adopts a distorted half chair conformation with ring puckering parameters are q2=0.3690(2) Å, phi2=77.40(4)°, q3= -0.1627(3) Å, QT= 0.4033(3) Å and θ= 113.79(4)° [128]. The atomic coordinates of bonded, non-bonded, and various contact contributions on the Hirshfeld surface are given in Table 2.4.9-11, respectively.

Crystal Packing Features

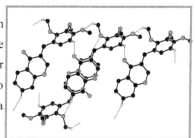

In the crystal packing each molecule is arranged in a molecular sheet along the diagonal of the unit cell in the 'ca' plane. The molecule at x,y, and z is connected to four of its adjacent symmetry related molecules forming two strands running in the opposite direction resulting in a molecular sheet characterized by a ladder-like structure.

DFDB

The intensity data collection and structure refinement details are listed in Table 2.5.1. The isotropic, anisotropic displacement parameters, hydrogen coordinates, and least squares planes are listed in Table 2.5.2-7. The ORTEP plot representing the molecular structure drawn at a 30% probability level [Fig. 2.2], packing of the molecules within the unit cell viewed along the 'b' axis [Fig. 2.3]. In the title compound, experimentally estimated C-C and C=C bond distances of the phenyl ring C1-C6 and C11-C16 are in the range 1.387(1)-1.405(2) and 1.366(2)-1.404(2) Å, respectively, and the other C-C single bond distances 1.473(1)-1.510(1) Å, C=C [1.340(2) Å], C-O bond distances 1.369(1)-1.427(1) (Å), and C=O [1.220(1) Å] distance of the chromenone ring [Table 2.5.5] [126,127]. The torsion angle C10-C8-C9-O2=142.4(1)° and O1-C7-C8-C9= -168.9(1)°, indicates that is in +anti-clinal (+ac) and +anti-periplanar (+ap) orientation to the chromenone ring (Table 2.5.6). The dihedral angle between the mean planes of the phenyl rings is 51.7(2)°, which expresses the bisectional orientation between them (Table 2.5.8). The carbonyl oxygen O1 tends to be coplanar with the chromenone ring, which is revealed by the symmetry between the bond angles O1-

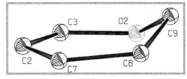

C7-C2 [122.4(1)°] and O1-C7-C8 [121.9(1)°]. In the title compound, the central cyclohexane ring adopts a sofa conformation with puckering parameters q2= 0.2416(2) Å, phi2 = -31.14(3)°, q3 = 0.2714(2) Å, QT = 0.3634(2) Å and Theta = 138.32(3)° [128]. The atomic coordinates of bonded, non-bonded, and various contact contributions on the Hirshfeld surface are given in Table 2.5.9-11, respectively.

Crystal Packing Features

The molecule at x, y, z is linked via C-H...O type hydrogen bonds with symmetric related molecule at x,1+y,z and x,2-y,1/2+z forming a chain described by C(16) [129] and remains parallel to [001] direction. The packing of the molecules in the unit cell viewed along the 'a' axis is shown in Fig. 2.3. Physical and chemical features of all compounds are given in Table 2.11

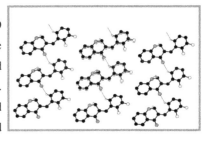

2.5 HIRSHFELD SURFACES ANALYSIS AND ENERGY FRAMEWORKS
INVESTIGATION
DBDB

For the title molecules, the Hirshfeld surface mapped over d_{norm} was quantified with the default setting of arbitrary unit range by using the validated Crystallographic Information File (CIF) as input to the Crystal Explorer 17.5. On rotation of the calculated plot Fig. 2.4(a), helps in identifying the bright-red spots near the methoxy hydrogen and carbonyl oxygen atoms indicate donors and acceptors of a potential C-H...O intermolecular interaction. The intensity of the red spots (bright, diminutive, and faint) can be utilized to specify the intermolecular interaction as potential hydrogen bonds, weak interactions, or short interatomic contacts. The Hirshfeld surfaces mapped over other surface properties namely shape-index and curvedness (Fig. 2.4b and d) can be effectively used to explain the role of weak intermolecular interactions such as C- H...π/π...π in stabilizing the crystal structure. The presence of adjacent blue and red regions (triangular shapes) within the ring systems on the Hirshfeld surface mapped over shape-index and the flat regions around the rings on the Hirshfeld surface mapped over curvedness is generally acknowledged as an indicator of C- H...π/π...π intermolecular contacts, but there are no such colored shapes either or flat regions over the generated Hirshfeld surface in the present study i.e the structure is devoid of C-H...π/π...π intermolecular contacts.

The calculated Hirshfeld surface of the title compounds can also be analyzed in terms of two-dimensional fingerprint plots. As shown in Fig.4, the resultant two-dimensional fingerprint plot which includes all intermolecular contacts is the sum of the delineated plots due to various specific interactions (Fig. 2.5a-e). In general, the main contribution to the overall surface arises from H...H contacts, whereas traditional hydrogen bonding always makes a relatively small percentage contribution to the overall surface. In Fig.2.5(b) and (d), the symmetrical forceps-like tips correspond to interactions H...C/C...H (15.2%) and H...O/O...H (13.9%) with d_i+ $d_e \approx 3$Å, which is slightly greater than the sum of the respective van der Waals radii, and indicative of the less likelihood for the C-H...π type of intermolecular contacts. The very weak π...π stacking interactions are evident from the fingerprint plot delineated into C...C (9%) contacts (Fig. 2.5c) as the rocket-like tip at d_e + d_i = 3.4Å. The fragment patches on the Hirshfeld surface provide a convenient way to identify the nearest neighbor coordination environment of a molecule.

The simulated energy frameworks were estimated to compare the topology of the intermolecular interactions in the title crystal. The pair-wise intermolecular interaction energies were calculated for a selected molecule in a cluster of molecules of radius 3.8Å, using an energy model CE-B3LYP (Fig. 2.6a and Table 2.6). In the energy frameworks, the individual energy components such as E_{ele}, E_{dis} and E_{tot} are depicted as cylinders in red, green, and blue colors, respectively, and with the radius of the corresponding cylinders proportional to the magnitude of interaction energy. The crystal packing of the title material is mainly stabilized by electrostatic and dispersive forces. These energies confirm that the interactions are predominantly dispersion based as is revealed by the energy-framework diagrams in Fig. 2.6a. Where the magnitude of the dispersion energies almost mirrors the total energies; the electrostatic term though not influential, but largely canceled by repulsion in each case.

MPDB

The Hirshfeld surfaces (HS) and 2D fingerprint plots were generated to explore and estimate the weak molecular interactions using the program Crystal Explorer 17.5 (Turner et al., 2017). In this work, the H-H contacts with de=di≈2Å contribute the most [43.8%] to the total Hirshfeld surface followed by the H-C [29.1%] interactions. The other contacts H-O (20.8%), C-C (5.0%), and C-O (0.9%) are also donated considerably to the total Hirshfeld surface as shown in Fig.2.8. The surface property shape-index is a tool to visualize the C-H...π stacking interactions through the adjacent red and blue triangles within the rings and in the present study the presence of such triangles clearly shows that the structure is stabilized also by C-H...π interactions [H-C (29.1%)]. The fragment patches [Fig. 2.7] on the Hirshfeld surface provide an easy way to investigate the nearest neighbor coordination environment of a molecule (coordination number), which is 22 for the present molecule. The pair-wise intermolecular interaction energies described by the cylinders connecting the centroid-centroid of the adjacent molecules were calculated for a selected molecule in a cluster of molecules of radius 3.8Å, using the energy model CE-B3LYP and expressed as a sum of four scaled energy components namely E_{elec}, E_{disp}, E_{pol}, and E_{rep}. In this work, the dispersion energy (E_{disp}) is observed to be the most contributing component to the total stabilizing energies than the remaining components (Fig.2.9 and Table 2.7).

TPDB

In the case of Hirshfeld surface is mapped over d_{norm}, d_i and d_e are the closest internal and external distances to the chosen point on the surface. The H-H contacts with $d_e = d_i$≈.2Å contribute the most [45.5%] to the total Hirshfeld surface followed by the C-H [14.8%] interactions. The other contacts O-C (0.7%), O-H (13.9%), H-O (11.8%), H-C(10.5%), C-O (0.9%), and O-O (0.6%) are also donating considerably to the total Hirshfeld surface shown in Fig.2.11. The shape-index of the Hirshfeld surface is a tool to visualize the π - π stacking interactions by the presence of adjacent red and blue triangles. The presence of such triangles clearly shows that there is π -π interactions in the title compound. Curvedness is a function of the root-mean-square curvature of the Hirshfeld surface, and it is used to define the nearest neighboring molecules in the crystal structure. The fragment patches [Fig.2.10] on the Hirshfeld

34

surface provide a convenient way to identify the nearest neighbor coordination environment of a molecule. The red regions on the surface of electrostatic potential indicate the positions of acceptor atoms O2 and O3 of the title compound. In this work, the dispersion energy (E_{disp}) is observed to be the most contributing component to the total stabilizing energies than the remaining components (Fig. 2.12 and Table 2.8).

TMDB

The Hirshfeld surface mapped over d_{norm}, d_i and d_e are the closest internal and external distances to the chosen point on the surface. In this work, the H-H contacts with $d_e = d_i \approx 2$Å contribute the most [51.0%] to the total Hirshfeld surface followed by the O-H [24.4%] interactions. The other contacts C-H (17.5%), C-C (4.9%) and O-C (2.2%) are also donating considerably to the total Hirshfeld surface shown in Fig.2.14. The shape-index of the Hirshfeld surface is a tool to visualize the π - π stacking interactions by the presence of adjacent red and blue triangles. The presence of such triangles clearly shows that there is π -π interactions in the title compound. Curvedness [Fig. 2.13] is a function of the root-mean-square curvature of the Hirshfeld surface and it is used to define the nearest neighboring molecules in the crystal structure. The red regions on the surface of electrostatic potential indicate the positions of acceptor atoms O2 and O3 of the title compound. In this work, the dispersion energy (E_{disp}) is observed to be the most contributing component to the total stabilizing energies than the remaining components (Fig.2.15 and Table 2.9).

DFDB

In this work, the C-C contacts with $d_e = d_i \approx 2$Å contribute the most [35.3%] to the total Hirshfeld surface followed by the C-F [19.7%] interactions. The other contacts C-O (14.1%), F-F (1.7%), F-C (15.1%), O-C (12.5%), O-O (1.4%) and O-F (0.2%) are also donated considerably to the total Hirshfeld surface is shown in Fig.2.17. The coordination environment of a molecule (coordination number), is 14 for the present molecule [Fig. 2.16]. The pair-wise intermolecular interaction energies described by the cylinders connecting the centroid-centroid of the adjacent molecules were calculated for a selected molecule in a cluster of molecules of radius 3.8Å, using the energy model CE-B3LYP and expressed as a sum of four scaled energy components namely E_{elec}, E_{disp}, E_{pol}, and E_{rep} is shown in Fig.2.18. In this work, the dispersion energy (E_{disp}) is observed to be the most contributing component to the total stabilizing energies than the remaining components (Fig. 2.18 and Table 2.10).

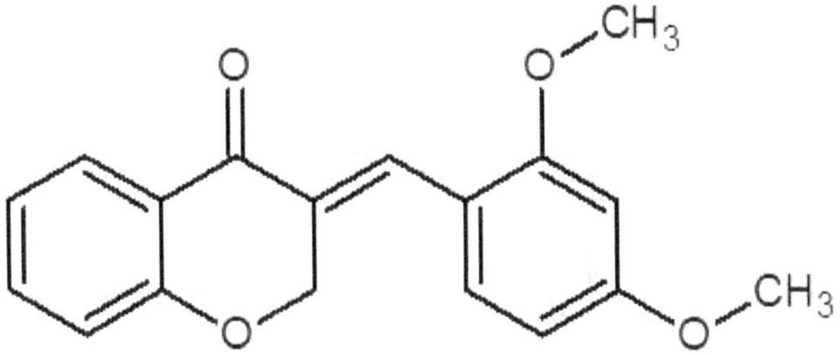

DBDB

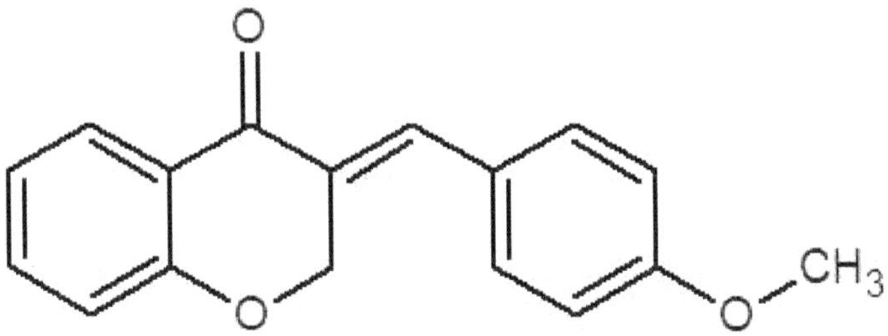

MPDB

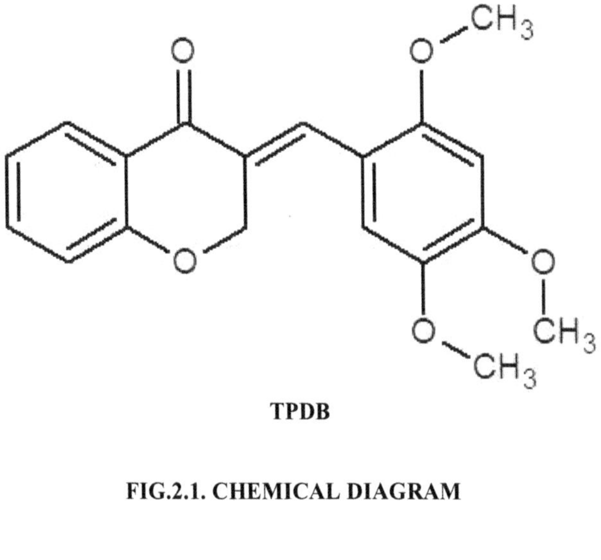

TPDB

FIG.2.1. CHEMICAL DIAGRAM

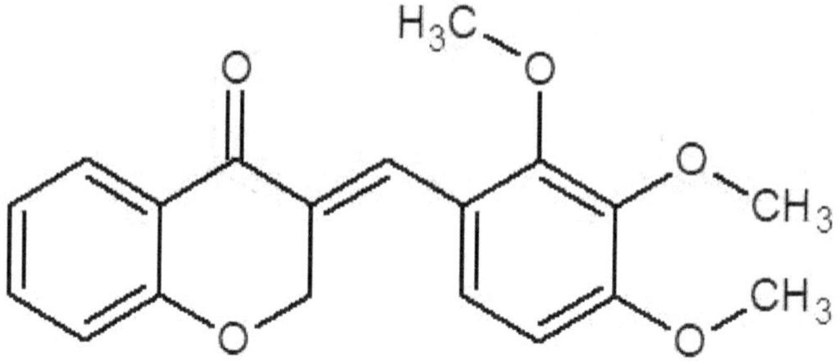

TMDB

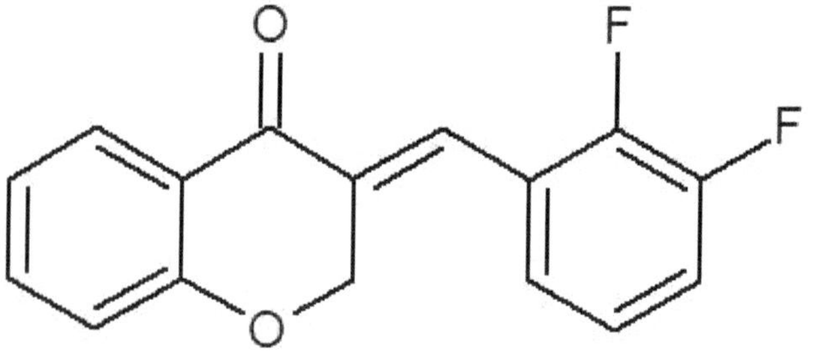

DFDB

FIG.2.1 CHEMICAL DIAGRAM

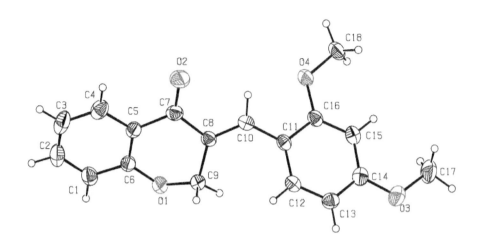

DBDB

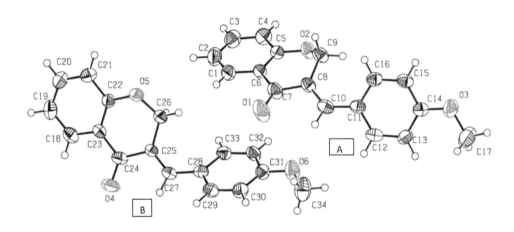

MPDB

FIG.2.2 ORTEP PLOTS OF COMPOUND WITH DISPLACEMENT ELLIPSOIDS

DRAWN AT 30% PROBABILITY LEVEL

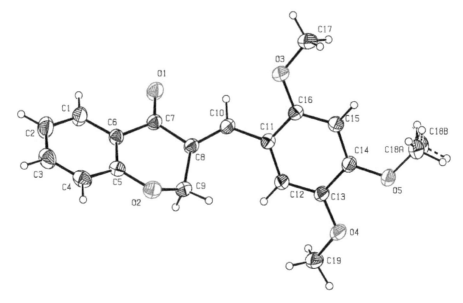

TPDB

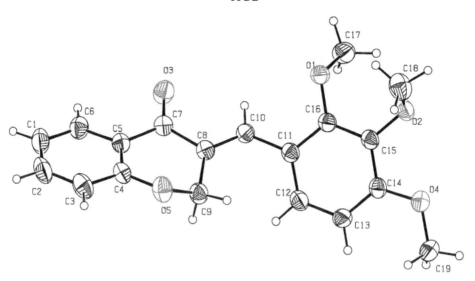

TMDB

FIG.2.2 ORTEP PLOTS OF COMPOUND WITH DISPLACEMENT ELLIPSOIDS DRAWN AT 30% PROBABILITY LEVEL

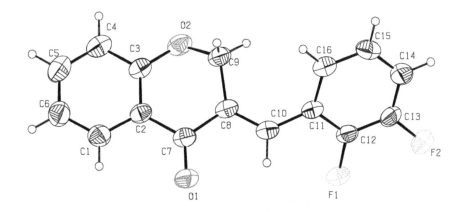

DFDB

FIG.2.2 ORTEP PLOT OF COMPOUND WITH DISPLACEMENT ELLIPSOIDS

DRAWN AT 30% PROBABILITY LEVEL

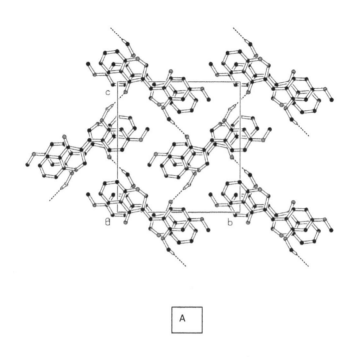

A

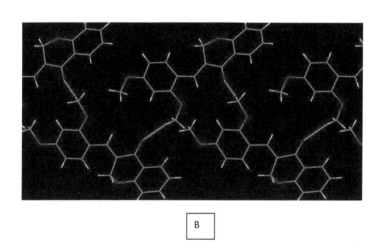

B

FIG.2.3 THE CRYSTAL PACKING OF DBDB, VIEWED ALONG 'a' AXIS.

B. HYDROGEN BONDING PATTERN

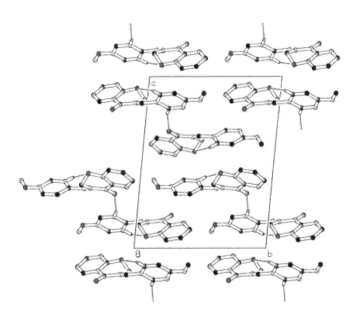

FIG.2.3 THE CRYSTAL PACKING OF MPDB, VIEWED ALONG 'c' AXIS. THE DASHED LINES INDICATE HYDROGEN BONDS

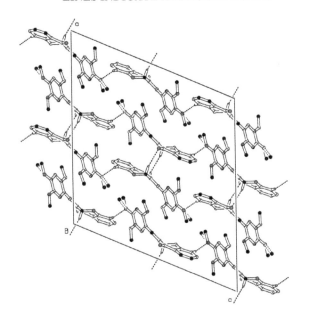

FIG.2.3 THE CRYSTAL PACKING OF COMPOUND TPDB, VIEWED ALONG 'a' AXIS. THE DASHED LINES INDICATE HYDROGEN BONDS

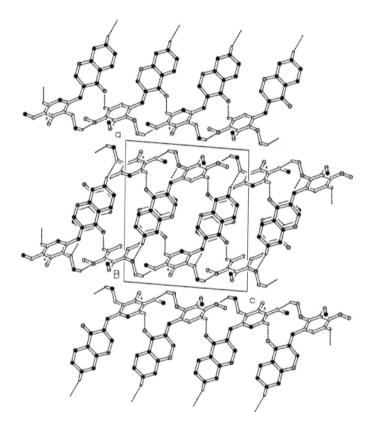

FIG.2.3 THE CRYSTAL PACKING OF COMPOUND TMDB, VIEWED ALONG 'b' AXIS. THE DASHED LINES INDICATE HYDROGEN BONDS

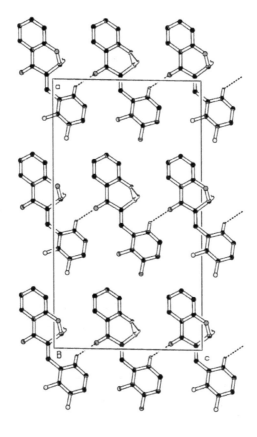

FIG.2.3 THE CRYSTAL PACKING OF COMPOUND DFDB, VIEWED ALONG 'b' AXIS.

THE DASHED LINES INDICATE HYDROGEN BONDS

Table 2.1.1

Crystal data and structure refinement details (DBDB)

Crystal Data	DBDB
Empirical formula	$C_{18}H_{16}O_4$
Temperature (K)	296(2)
Wavelength (Å)	0.71073
Crystal system	Orthorhombic
Space group	$P2_12_12_1$
Unit cell dimensions (Å,°)	$\alpha=\beta=\gamma = 90$ a =7.8756(5) b=13.4142(8) c=13.8440(8)
Volume (Å³)	1462.55(2)
Z	4
Density calculated (Mg/m³)	1.346
Absorption coefficient (mm⁻¹)	0.095
F(000)	624
Crystal size (mm)	0.200 x 0.200 x 0.150
Theta range for data collection (°)	2.943 to 26.415
Index ranges	$-9 \leq h \leq 9, -16 \leq k \leq 16, -17 \leq l \leq 17$
Reflections collected	35974
Independent reflections	2971 [R(int.) = 0.049]
Completeness to $\theta = 25.242°$	99.5 %
Refinement method	Full-matrix least-squares on F^2
Data / restraints / parameters	2971 / 0 / 199
Goodness-of-fit on F^2	1.095
Final R indices [I>2sigma(I)]	R1 = 0.046, wR2 = 0.126
R indices (all data)	R1 = 0.057, wR2 = 0.142
Absolute structure parameter	-0.4(3)
Extinction coefficient	n/a
Largest diff. peak and hole (e.Å⁻³)	0.20 and -0.18

Table 2.1.2

Atomic coordinates (x 10^4) and equivalent isotropic displacement parameters ($\text{Å}^2 \text{x} 10^3$) for non- hydrogen atom with (e s d) in parentheses

Atom	x	y	z	$U_{(eq)}$
O1	2939(3)	8376(2)	6753(2)	56(1)
O4	3058(3)	6289(2)	2984(2)	59(1)
O3	4434(4)	3119(2)	4452(2)	72(1)
O2	5013(4)	9335(2)	4221(2)	78(1)
C9	4026(4)	7685(2)	6256(2)	50(1)
C16	3689(3)	5704(2)	3707(2)	45(1)
C12	5048(4)	5647(2)	5244(2)	48(1)
C13	5072(4)	4623(3)	5211(2)	51(1)
C5	4150(4)	9711(2)	5808(2)	47(1)
C10	4423(4)	7299(2)	4481(2)	45(1)
C15	3679(4)	4671(2)	3668(2)	50(1)
C11	4352(3)	6220(2)	4505(2)	42(1)
C7	4568(4)	9027(2)	5010(2)	50(1)
C14	4369(4)	4135(2)	4424(2)	51(1)
C8	4337(4)	7955(2)	5214(2)	44(1)
C6	3294(4)	9366(2)	6617(2)	48(1)
C1	2697(4)	10028(3)	7312(2)	60(1)
C18	2467(5)	5813(3)	2125(2)	67(1)
C2	2993(5)	11027(3)	7200(3)	69(1)
C4	4462(5)	10736(2)	5726(3)	63(1)
C3	3898(5)	11382(3)	6420(4)	76(1)
C17	3746(6)	2587(3)	3643(3)	86(1)

$U_{(eq)} = 1/3 \; \Sigma_i \Sigma_j U_{ij} a_i^* \; a_j^* \; a_i a_j$

Table 2.1.3

Anisotropic displacement parameters ($\mathring{A}^2$ x 10^3) for non-hydrogen atoms with

(e s d) in parentheses

Atom	U_{11}	U_{22}	U_{33}	U_{23}	U_{13}	U_{12}
O1	72(1)	49(1)	46(1)	-2(1)	8(1)	2(1)
O4	74(1)	57(1)	46(1)	-11(1)	-17(1)	12(1)
O3	89(2)	48(1)	80(2)	-1(1)	-6(2)	-5(1)
O2	113(2)	64(2)	56(1)	11(1)	11(2)	-19(2)
C9	65(2)	43(1)	42(1)	-1(1)	2(1)	3(1)
C16	40(1)	53(2)	41(1)	-7(1)	-1(1)	7(1)
C12	46(1)	55(2)	41(1)	-4(1)	-1(1)	0(1)
C13	49(2)	57(2)	49(2)	7(1)	4(1)	3(1)
C5	45(1)	43(1)	52(2)	0(1)	-16(1)	-1(1)
C10	45(1)	52(2)	39(1)	1(1)	0(1)	-2(1)
C15	45(1)	53(2)	52(2)	-11(1)	1(1)	-2(1)
C11	37(1)	50(2)	39(1)	-6(1)	4(1)	1(1)
C7	55(2)	51(2)	45(2)	5(1)	-8(1)	-8(1)
C14	50(2)	47(2)	58(2)	-3(1)	9(2)	-3(1)
C8	45(1)	46(2)	39(1)	-1(1)	-5(1)	-2(1)
C6	50(2)	45(2)	49(2)	-3(1)	-17(1)	4(1)
C1	58(2)	63(2)	58(2)	-13(2)	-14(2)	12(2)
C18	82(2)	72(2)	46(2)	-17(2)	-16(2)	15(2)
C2	62(2)	57(2)	88(3)	-26(2)	-22(2)	14(2)
C4	61(2)	47(2)	81(2)	3(2)	-16(2)	-7(2)
C3	71(2)	42(2)	115(3)	-9(2)	-22(2)	1(2)
C17	109(3)	49(2)	100(3)	-16(2)	-14(3)	-6(2)

The anisotropic displacement factor exponent takes the form:

$$-2\pi^2[\,h^2a^{*2}U_{11} + ... + 2\,h\,k\,a^*\,b^*\,U_{12}\,]$$

Table 2.1.4

Hydrogen coordinates (x 10^4) and isotropic displacement

parameters (Å^2x 10^3)

Atom	x	y	z	$U_{(eq)}$
H9A	3518	7027	6283	60
H9B	5108	7654	6590	60
H12	5510	5968	5779	57
H13	5558	4260	5712	62
H10	4545	7579	3870	54
H15	3213	4343	3139	60
H1	2103	9794	7847	72
H18A	2061	6308	1680	100
H18B	3382	5448	1833	100
H18C	1561	5363	2283	100
H2	2578	11473	7657	83
H4	5058	10980	5195	75
H3	4125	12060	6366	91
H17A	3867	1883	3748	129
H17B	2565	2749	3572	129
H17C	4346	2774	3067	129

Table 2.1.5

Selected Bond lengths [Å] and angles [°] involving non- hydrogen atom with (e s d) in parentheses

Atoms	Bond distances (Å)	Atoms	Bond angles (°)	Atoms	Bond angles (°)
O1-C6	1.371(4)	C6-O1-C9	116.0(2)	C10-C8-C9	124.9(3)
O1-C9	1.436(4)	C16-O4-C18	118.2(2)	C7-C8-C9	116.0(3)
O4-C16	1.366(4)	C14-O3-C17	117.4(3)	O1-C6-C5	122.2(3)
O4-C18	1.428(4)	O1-C9-C8	113.6(2)	O1-C6-C1	117.0(3)
O3-C14	1.364(4)	O4-C16-C15	122.9(3)	C5-C6-C1	120.7(3)
O3-C17	1.434(5)	O4-C16-C11	115.4(2)	C2-C1-C6	119.2(4)
O2-C7	1.220(4)	C15-C16-C11	121.7(3)	C1-C2-C3	121.0(3)
C9-C8	1.508(4)	C13-C12-C11	122.1(3)	C3-C4-C5	120.4(4)
C2-C3	1.3789(6)	C12-C13-C14	119.5(3)		
C4-C3	1.368(5)	C6-C5-C4	118.6(3)		
C16-C15	1.387(4)	C6-C5-C7	120.7(3		
C16-C11	1.403(4)	C8-C10-C11	129.4(3)		
C12-C13	1.374(5)	C4-C5-C7	120.7(3)		
C12-C11	1.393(4)	C14-C15-C16	119.3(3)		
C13-C14	1.386(4)	C12-C11-C16	117.0(3)		
C5-C6	1.386(4)	C12-C11-C10	123.6(3)		
C5-C4	1.403(4)	C16-C11-C10	119.2(3)		
C5-C7	1.473(4)	O2-C7-C5	121.7(3)		
C10-C8	1.345(4)	O2-C7-C8	122.5(3)		
C10-C11	1.450(4)	C5-C7-C8	115.8(2)		
C15- C14	1.381(4)	O3-C14-C15	123 8(3)		
C7-C8	1.476(4)	O3-C14-C13	115.8(3)		
C6-C1	1.392(4)	C15-C14-C13	120.4(3)		
C1-C2	1.369(5)	C4-C3-C2	120.0(3)		

Table 2.1.6

Torsion angles [°] with (e s d) in parentheses

Atoms	Torsion angles (°)	Atoms	Torsion angles (°)
C11-C10-C8-C9	-4.17(1)	C6 -O1 -C9 -C8	-45.97(1)
C11-C10-C8-C7	175.5(2)	C9 -O1 -C6 -C5	24.03(2)
C16-C15-C14-O3	-179.41(1)	C9 -O1 -C6 -C1	-158.51(1)
C16-C15-C14-C3	-0.39(2)	C18-O4 -C16-C15	-4.24(2)
O2-C7-C8 -C9	171.66(2)	C18-O4-C16-C11	175.97(1)
O2-C7-C8-C10	-8.04(1)	C17-O3-C14-C13	-178.91(2)
C5-C7-C8 -C9	-11.08(1)	C17 -O3-C14 -C15	0.16(1)
C5-C7-C8-C10	169.23(2)	O1-C9-C8-C10	-141.04(2)
O1-C6-C1-C2	-178.87(2)	O1-C9-C8-C7	39.29(1)
C5-C6-C1-C2	-1.37(3)	O4 -C16 -C15-C14	178.93(2)
C6 -C1-C2-C3	-1.17(1)	C11 -C16 -C15 -C14	-1.3(1)
C1-C2-C3-C4	2.35(1)	O4 -C16 -C11 -C10	-3.91(1)
C5-C4-C3-C2	-0.98(2)	C15 -C16 -C11-C12	1.89(2)
C4-C5-C7-O2	-8.39(2)	C15 -C16 -C11-C10	176.3(1)
C4-C5-C7-C8	174.32(2)	C6 -C5-C7-C8	-11.77(1)
C7-C5-C6 -O1	6.12(1)	C11-C12-C13-C14	-0.77(2)
C7-C5-C6 -C1	-171.37(1)	C13-C12-C11-C16	-0.84(1)
C4-C5-C6-O1	-179.96(2)	O4 -C16 -C11 -C12	-178.32(2)
C4 -C5-C6-C1	2.67(2)	C13 -C12-C11-C10	-175(1)
C7-C5-C4-C3	172.53(1)	C12-C13 -C14 -O3	-179.49(2)
C6-C5-C4-C3	-1.49(2)	C12-C13 -C14-C15	1.41(1)
C8-C10 -C11-C16	150.56(1)	C6 -C5-C7-O2	165.52(1)
C8-C10-C11-C12	-35.41(2)		

Table 2.1.7

Least-square planes through the various groups of atoms and deviations (Å) for the compound.
Equation of the plane: $m1x + m2y + m3z = d$, where m1, m2, and m3 are direction cosines.

*Starred atoms are included in the plane calculations

plane	m₁	m₂	m₃	D	Atom	Deviation (Å)
1	0.0144	-0.9989	-0.0426	-3.3485	C4 *	0.0278(1)
					C5 *	0.1184(2)
					C7 *	-0.0945(2)
					C8*	-0.0725(2)
					C9*	0.03343(1)
					C10*	-0.3931(2)
					O5	-0.1751(1)
2	0.7794	-0.5454	-0.3080	4.8206	C13*	0.0288(1)
					C12*	-0.0061(1)
					C11*	-0.0283(2)
					C16*	0.0395(2)
					C15*	-0.0224(2)
					C14*	-0.0103(1)
					O1	0.1034(1)
3	0.7794	-0.5454	-0.3080	4.82076	C11*	-0.0283(1)
					C12*	0.0061(2)
					C13*	0.0288(2)
					C14*	-0.0103(1)
					C15*	-0.0224(1)
					C16*	0.0395(2)
					O2	-0.0598(2)

Table 2.1.8

Dihedral angle (°) formed by LSQ- planes for the compound with

(e s d) in parentheses

Plane-Plane	Angle (°)
1-2	55.30(1)
2-3	51.66(1)

Table 2.1.9

Geometry of the Hydrogen bonds [Å, °]

D-H...A	d(D-H)	d(H...A)	d(D...A)	<(DHA)
C18-H18B ...O2 #1	0.96	2.44	3.368(5)	162

Symmetry code: #1 1-x,-1/2+y,1/2-z

Table 2.1.10

Geometry of the non- bonded interaction [Å, °].

D-H...A	d(D-H)	d(H...A)	d(D...A)	<(DHA)
C10-H10 ...O2	0.93	2.43	2.794(4)	103

Table 2.1.11

Various contact contributions (%) in Hirshfeld surface

Inter contacts	Percentage (%)	Ratio (%)	Nature of Structure
ALL	100		
H-H	50.1		
H-C/C-H	22.3		
C-O/O-C	15.2	C-H/C-C=2.47	β structure
C-C	9.0		
O-C	3.3		

Table 2.2.1

Crystal data and structure refinement details (MPDB)

Crystal Data	MPDB	
Empirical formula	$C_{17}H_{14}O_3$	
Formula weight	266.28	
Temperature (K)	293(2)	
Wavelength (Å)	0.71073	
Crystal system	Triclinic	
Space group	P $\bar{1}$	
Unit cell dimensions (Å,°)	a = 7.6435(5)	α=83.068(5)
	b = 12.5167(8)	β=87.333(8)
	c = 14.8087(10)	γ = 75.846(2)
Volume (Å^3)	1363.50(3)	
Z	4	
Density (calculated) (Mg/m^3)	1.297	
Absorption coefficient (mm^{-1})	0.089	
F(000)	560	
Crystal size (mm)	0.200 x 0.200 x 0.150	
Theta range for data collection (°)	2.859 to 24.994	
Index ranges	-9≤h≤9, -14≤k≤14, -17≤l≤17	
Reflections collected	35157	
Independent reflections	3515[R(int) = 0.059]	
Completeness to theta = 24.994°	99.8 %	
Refinement method	Full-matrix least-squares on F^2	
Data / restraints / parameters	35157 / 0 / 364	
Goodness-of-fit on F^2	1.083	
Final R indices [I>2sigma (I)]	R1 = 0.070, wR2 = 0.261	
R indices (all data)	R1 = 0.155, wR2 = 0.296	
Extinction coefficient	n/a	
Largest diff. peak and hole (e.Å^{-3})	0.36 and -0.36	

Table 2.2.2

Atomic coordinates (x 10^4) and equivalent isotropic displacement parameters(Å^2x10^3) for non-hydrogen atom with (e s d) in parentheses

Atom	x	y	z	$U_{(eq)}$
C18A	7432(1)	130(2)	3078(2)	85(3)
C18B	7266(3)	240(4)	2831(3)	79(4)
C1	5694(1)	7433(3)	6551(1)	57(1)
C2	5738(1)	7235(3)	7195(1)	71(1)
C3	5920(1)	5481(4)	7514(1)	68(1)
C4	6046(1)	3924(3)	7198(1)	58(1)
C5	5985(1)	4108(2)	6539(1)	45(1)
C6	5815(1)	5869(2)	6214(1)	43(1)
C7	5831(1)	6147(2)	5552(1)	44(1)
C8	5974(1)	4394(2)	5250(1)	43(1)
C9	5857(1)	2528(2)	5529(1)	51(1)
C10	6225(1)	4625(2)	4797(1)	45(1)
C11	6421(1)	3198(2)	4430(1)	44(1)
C12	6100(1)	1477(2)	4180(1)	46(1)
C13	6281(1)	236(2)	3794(1)	45(1)
C14	6797(1)	713(2)	3647(1)	46(1)
C15	7125(1)	2380(2)	3896(1)	48(1)
C16	6936(1)	3625(2)	4278(1)	45(1)
C17	7683(1)	6010(3)	4318(1)	71(1)
C19	5407(1)	-1811(3)	3543(1)	60(1)
O1	5758(1)	7734(2)	5289(1)	63(1)
O2	6119(1)	2528(2)	6247(1)	58(1)
O3	7230(1)	5310(2)	4534(1)	63(1)
O4	5988(1)	-1433(2)	3516(1)	62(1)
O5	6927(1)	-544(2)	3240(1)	62(1)

$U_{(eq)} = 1/3\ \Sigma_i\Sigma_j U_{ij}a_i{}^*\ a_j{}^*\ a_i a_j$

55

Table 2.2.3

Anisotropic displacement parameters (Å^2 x 10^3) for non-hydrogen atoms
with (e s d) in parentheses

Atom	U_{11}	U_{22}	U_{33}	U_{23}	U_{13}	U_{12}
C18A	100(1)	77(1)	114(2)	-31(1)	80(1)	-20(1)
C18B	83(1)	92(1)	89(1)	-30(2)	63(1)	-23(1)
C1	71(1)	53(1)	51(1)	-4(1)	26(1)	7(1)
C2)	89(1)	76(1)	52(1)	-11(1)	32(1)	1(1)
C3	73(1)	90(2)	40(1)	-5(1)	21(1)	-15(1)
C4	57(1)	66(1)	46(1)	12(1)	14(1)	-8(1)
C5	42(1)	47(1)	45(1)	4(1)	15(1)	-3(1)
C6	44(1)	43(1)	40(1)	0(1)	16(1)	1(1)
C7	52(1)	36(1)	45(1)	0(1)	20(1)	3(1)
C8	49(1)	35(1)	44(1)	-1(1)	18(1)	1(1)
C9	64(1)	36(1)	58(1)	-2(1)	27(1)	-2(1)
C10	53(1)	38(1)	45(1)	-5(1)	19(1)	-2(1)
C11	50(1)	41(1)	42(1)	-5(1)	18(1)	-2(1)
C12	47(1)	47(1)	49(1)	-9(1)	23(1)	-7(1)
C13	45(1)	43(1)	48(1)	-10(1)	19(1)	-6(1)
C14	46(1)	44(1)	49(1)	-8(1)	20(1)	-1(1)
C15	44(1)	49(1)	53(1)	-6(1)	22(1)	-6(1)
C16	47(1)	42(1)	44(1)	-6(1)	16(1)	-7(1)
C17	73(1)	55(1)	94(2)	-14(1)	41(1)	-21(1)
C19	55(1)	55(1)	74(1)	-14(1)	28(1)	-15(1)
O1	102(1)	38(1)	58(1)	6(1)	40(1)	12(1)
O2	76(1)	41(1)	57(1)	11(1)	27(1)	9(1)
O3	70(1)	52(1)	75(1)	-22(1)	37(1)	-23(1)
O4	61(1)	54(1)	81(1)	-30(1)	39(1)	-20(1)
O5	65(1)	56(1)	80(1)	-24(1)	45(1)	-11(1)

The anisotropic displacement factor exponent takes the form:

$$-2\pi^2[\,h^2 a^{*2} U_{11} + ... + 2\,h\,k\,a^*\,b^*\,U_{12}\,]$$

Table 2.2.4

Hydrogen coordinates (x 10^4) and isotropic displacement

parameters ($Å^2$ x 10^3)

Atom	x	y	z	$U_{(eq)}$
H18A	7800	-126	3473	128
H18B	7378	1117	2872	128
H18C	7467	-1086	2778	128
H18D	7090	1449	2642	118
H18E	7231	-657	2483	118
H18F	7692	411	3107	118
H1	5582	8615	6338	69
H2	5647	8267	7414	85
H3	5956	5355	7952	82
H4	6170	2761	7421	70
H9A	5416	2313	5376	62
H9B	6034	1479	5368	62
H10	6283	5899	4702	54
H12	5758	1168	4277	55
H15	7473	2667	3808	57
H17A	7807	7277	4494	106
H17B	7519	6066	3843	106
H17C	8034	5167	4468	106
H19A	5255	-3024	3333	91
H19B	5124	-807	3316	91
H19C	5447	-1859	3996	91

Table 2.2.5

Selected Bond lengths [Å] and angles [°] involving non- hydrogen atom with (e s d) in parentheses

Atoms	Bond lengths	Atoms	Bond angles	Atoms	Bond angles
C18-O5	1.391(1)	C2-C1-C6	120.3(2)	C29-C30-C31	119.9(2)
C18-O5	1.51(2)	C3-C2-C1	118.6(2)	O6-C31-C32	116.5(2)
C1-C2	1.378(3)	C4-C3-C2	122.6(2)	O6-C31-C30	125.3(2)
C1-C6	1.402(2)	C3-C4-C5	118.5(1)	C33-C32-C31	121.6(2)
C2-C3	1.388(3)	O2-C5-C4	116.8(1)	C5-O2-C9	115.3(2)
C3-C4	1.375(3)	O2-C5-C6	122.1(1)	C14-O3-C17	119.0(2)
C4-C5	1.399(2)	C4-C5-C6	121.0(1)	C22-O5-C26	115.2(2)
C5-O2	1.365(2)	C5-C6-C1	118.8(2)	C31-O6-C34	119.1(1)
C5-C6	1.394(2)	C5-C6-C7	120.2(1)		
C6-C7	1.472(2)	C1-C6-C7	120.8(1)		
C7-O1	1.2250(2)	O1-C7-C6	121.9(1)		
C7-C8	1.484(2)	O1-C7-C8	122.0(2)		
C8-C10	1.340(2)	C6-C7-C8	116.1(2)		
C8-C9	1.502(2)	C10-C8-C7	119.5(1)		
C9-O2	1.450(2)	C10-C8-C9	125.3(1)		
C10-C11	1.456(2)	C7-C8-C9	115.1(1)		
C11-C16	1.402(2)	O2-C9-C8	111.6(1)		
C11-C12	1.408(2)	C8-C10-C11	129.3(1)		
C12-C13	1.380(2)	C12-C11-C16	115.7(2)		
C13-O4	1.3659(2)	C12-C11-C10	120.0(1)		
C13-C14	1.406(2)	C16-C11-C10	124.2(2)		
C14-O5	1.3619(2)	C13-C12-C11	123.6(1)		
C14-C15	1.397(2)	C12-C13-C14	119.1(1)		
C15-C16	1.372(2)	O3-C14-C15	116.6(1)		
C16-O3	1.3653(2)	O3-C14-C13	124.9(1)		
C17-O3	1.445(2)	C15-C14-C13	118.5(1)		
C19-O4	1.412(2)	C16-C15-C14	122.0(1)		

C14-O3	1.369(1)	C15-C16-C11	121.1(1)
C18-C23	1.398(1)	C23-C18-C19	121.8(2)
C18-C19	1.402(2)	C20-C19-C18	118.0(1)
C19-C20	1.396(1)	C21-C20-C19	122.1(1)
C20-C21	1.369(1)	C20-C21-C22	119.1(1)
C21-C22	1.402(1)	O5-C22-C21	117.1(1)
C22-O5	1.367(1)	O5-C22-C23	121.7(1)
C22-C23	1.404(1)	C21-C22-C23	121.1(1)
C23-C24	1.466(1)	C18-C23-C22	117.9(2)
C24-O4	1.234(1)	C18-C23-C24	121.8(1)
C24-C25	1.496(2)	C22-C23-C24	120.2(1)
C25-C27	1.352(2)	O4-C24-C23	121.6(2)
C25-C26	1.503(1)	O4-C24-C25	121.9(1)
C26-O5	1.467(1)	C23-C24-C25	116.5(2)
C27-C28	1.457(1)	C27-C25-C24	119.7(2)
C28-C29	1.411(2)	C27-C25-C26	124.9(1)
C28-C33	1.416(1)	C24-C25-C26	115.3(1)
C29-C30	1.379(2)	O5-C26-C25	112.4(1)
C30-C31	1.408(2)	C25-C27-C28	129.4(1)
C31-O6	1.357(2)	C29-C28-C33	115.8(1)
C31-C32	1.389(1)	C29-C28-C27	119.4(2)
C32-C33	1.377(1)	C33-C28-C27	124.7(1)
C34-O6	1.432(1)	C30-C29-C28	122.9(1)

Table 2.2.6

Torsion angles [°] with (e s d) in parentheses

Atoms	Torsion angles	Atoms	Torsion angles
C17-O1-C16-C15	68.7(1)	O2-C15-C14-O4	0.8(1)
C17-O1-C16-C11	-114.4(1)	C16-C15-C14-O4	179.1(1)
C18-O2-C15-C16	71.7(2)	O2-C15-C14-C13	-179.9(1)
C18-O2-C15-C14	-110.1(1)	C16-C15-C14-C13	-1.7(1)
O1-C16-C15-O2	1.9(2)	C7-C8-C10-C11	-177.6(1)
C11-C16-C15-O2	-175.0(1)	C9-C8-C10-C11	1.7(1)
O1-C16-C15-C14	-176.4(1)	O1-C16-C11-C12	176.0(2)
C11-C16-C15-C14	6.8(2)	C15-C16-C11-C12	-7.1(1)
O3-C7-C5-C4	-164.9(1)	O1-C16-C11-C10	-2.2(1)
C8-C7-C5-C4	14.3(2)	C15-C16-C11-C10	174.6(1)
O3-C7-C5-C6	10.5(1)	C8-C10-C11-C12	37.2(1)
C8-C7-C5-C6	-170.4(1)	C8-C10-C11-C16	-144.6(2)
O3-C7-C8-C10	5.9(1)	C4-C5-C6-C1	0.5(1)
C5-C7-C8-C10	-173.2(1)	C7-C5-C6-C1	-174.9(2)
O3-C7-C8-C9	-173.4(2)	C9-O5-C4-C5	-28.7(1)
C5-C7-C8-C9	7.5(1)	C9-O5-C4-C3	153.3(1)
C19-O4-C14-C13	-2.5(2)	C6-C5-C4-O5	-179.6(1)
C19-O4-C14-C15	176.7(2)	C4-C3-C2-C1	-0.1(1)
C7-C5-C4-O5	-4.1(2)	O5-C4-C3-C2	179.5(1)
C6-C5-C4-C3	-1.7(2)	C5-C4-C3-C2	1.5(2)
C7-C5-C4-C3	173.8(2)	C5-C6-C1-C2	0.8(2)
C16-C11-C12-C13	2.5(2)	C6-C1-C2-C3	-1.0(2)
C10-C11-C12-C13	-179.4(1)	C15-C14-C13-C12	-2.9(2)
C4-O5-C9-C8	49.3(2)	O4-C14-C13-C12	176.3(1)
C10-C8-C9-O5	142.4(1)		
C7-C8-C9-O5	-38.3(2)		
C11-C12-C13-C14	2.5(1)		

Table 2.2.7

Least-square planes through the various groups of atoms and deviations (Å) for the compound. Equation of the plane: $m_1x + m_2y + m_3z = d$ where m_1, m_2, and m_3 are direction cosines. *Starred atoms are included in the plane calculations.

plane	m_1	m_2	m_3	D	Atom	Deviation (Å)
1	-0.4926	0.1092	-0.0863	-4.8036	C7 *	0.0953(1)
					C6 *	-0.1089(2)
					C5 *	-0.0560(2)
					C9*	-0.3636(2)
					C8*	0.1341(1)
					O2	0.1377(1)
2	0.4748	-0.1232	-0.8714	0.1634	C12*	-0.0063(1)
					C11*	0.0090(1)
					C16*	-0.0048(2)
					C15*	0.0015(2)
					C14*	-0.0030(2)
					C13*	0.0093(1)
					C12*	-0.0063(1)
					O3	0.0040(1)
3	0.4867	-0.1156	-0.8658	-3.4365	C24*	-0.1002(1)
					C23*	0.1146(1)
					C22*	0.0594(2)
					C26*	0.3478(1)
					C25*	-0.1182(2)
					O5	-0.1464(1)
4	-0.4494	0.1333	-0.8832	-4.7079	C29*	0.0145(1)
					C28*	-0.0054(1)
					C33*	-0.0027(1)
					C32*	0.0058(1)
					C30*	-0.0108(1)
					C31*	0.0003(1)
					O6	0.0139(1)

Table 2.2.8

Dihedral angle (°) formed by LSQ- planes for the compound with

(e s d) in parentheses

Plane-Plane	Angle (°)
1-2	59.6
1-3	60.3
2-4	57.3
3-4	57.9

Table 2.2.9

Geometry of the inter molecular hydrogen bond (Å, °)

D-H...A	d(D-H)	d(H...A)	d(D...A)	<(DHA)
C12-H12...O2 #1	0.93	2.55	3.408(7)	154
C16-H16...O4 #2	0.93	2.54	3.447(8)	165
C29-H29...O5 #3	0.93	2.54	3.422(7)	158

Symmetry Code = #1 1-x, 1-y,1-z ; #2 x,-y,1/2+z; #3 -1+x,y,z

Table 2.2.10

Geometry of the non- bonded Interaction [Å, °]

D-H...A	d(D-H)	d(H...A)	d(D...A)	<(DHA)
C10-H10...O1	0.93	2.48	2.837(8)	103
C27-H27...O4	0.93	2.47	2.832(8)	103

Table 2.2.11

Various contact contributions (%) in Hirshfeld surface

Inter contacts	Percentage (%)	Ratio (%)	Nature of Structure
ALL	100		
H-H	43.8		
H-C/C-H	29.1		
H-O/O-H	20.8	C-H/C-C = 5.82	Herringbone
C-C	5.0		structure
O-C/C-O	0.9		
O-O	0.3		

Table 2.3.1

Crystal data and structure refinement details (TPDB)

Crystal Data	TPDB	
Empirical formula	$C_{19}H_{18}O_5$	
Formula weight	326.33	
Temperature (K)	296(2)	
Wavelength (Å)	0.71073	
Crystal system	Monoclinic	
Space group	C2/c	
Unit cell dimensions (Å,°)	a=23.481(3)	β= 112.43(3)
	b=6.9443(1)	
	c=21.853(3)	
Volume (Å^3)	3293.6(8)	
Z	8	
Density (calculated) (Mg/m^3)	1.316	
Absorption coefficient (mm^{-1})	0.095	
F(000)	1376	
Crystal size (mm)	0.200 x 0.200 x 0.180	
Theta range for data collection (°)	3.080 to 36.347	
Index ranges	$-38 \leq h \leq 39, -11 \leq k \leq 11, -36 \leq l \leq 36$	
Reflections collected	46853	
Independent reflections	7959 [R(int) = 0.0573]	
Completeness to theta = 25.242°	99.4 %	
Refinement method	Full-matrix least-squares on F^2	
Data / restraints / parameters	7959 / 0 / 231	
Goodness-of-fit on F^2	1.062	
Final R indices [I>2sigma(I)]	R1 = 0.060, wR2 = 0.177	
R indices (all data)	R1 = 0.130, wR2 = 0.227	
Extinction coefficient	n/a	
Largest diff. peak and hole (e.Å^{-3})	0.24 and -0.33	

Table 2.3.2

Atomic coordinates (x 10^4) and equivalent isotropic displacement parameters (Å^2 x 10^3) for non- hydrogen atom with (e s d) in parentheses

Atom	x	y	z	$U_{(eq)}$
C18A	7432(8)	-130(2)	3078(2)	85(3)
C18B	7266(3)	240(1)	2831(1)	79(2)
C1	5694(1)	7433(3)	6551(1)	57(1)
C2	5738(1)	7235(3)	7195(1)	71(1)
C3	5920(1)	5481(4)	7514(1)	68(1)
C4	6046(1)	3924(3)	7198(1)	58(1)
C5	5985(1)	4108(2)	6539(1)	45(1)
C6	5815(1)	5869(2)	6214(1)	43(1)
C7	5831(1)	6147(2)	5552(1)	44(1)
C8	5974(1)	4394(2)	5250(1)	43(1)
C9	5857(1)	2528(2)	5529(1)	51(1)
C10	6225(1)	4625(2)	4797(1)	45(1)
C11	6421(1)	3198(2)	4430(1)	44(1)
C12	6100(1)	1477(2)	4180(1)	46(1)
C13	6281(1)	236(2)	3794(1)	45(1)
C14	6797(1)	713(2)	3647(1)	46(1)
C15	7125(1)	2380(2)	3896(1)	48(1)
C16	6936(1)	3625(2)	4278(1)	45(1)
C17	7683(1)	6010(3)	4318(1)	71(1)
C19	5407(1)	-1811(3)	3543(1)	60(1)
O1	5758(1)	7734(2)	5289(1)	63(1)
O2	6119(1)	2528(2)	6247(1)	58(1)
O3	7230(1)	5310(2)	4534(1)	63(1)
O4	5988(1)	-1433(2)	3516(1)	62(1)
O5	6927(1)	-544(2)	3240(1)	62(1)

$U_{(eq)} = 1/3 \ \Sigma_i\Sigma_j \ U_{ij}a_i^* \ a_j^* \ a_ia_j$

Table 2.3.3

Anisotropic displacement parameters ($\mathring{A}^2 \times 10^3$) for non-hydrogen atoms with (e s d) in parentheses

Atom	U_{11}	U_{22}	U_{33}	U_{23}	U_{13}	U_{12}
C18A	100(1)	77(4)	114(1)	-31(1)	80(1)	-20(1)
C18B	83(2)	92(1)	89(2)	-30(2)	63(2)	-23(2)
C1	71(1)	53(1)	51(1)	-4(1)	26(1)	7(1)
C2	89(1)	76(1)	52(1)	-11(1)	32(1)	1(1)
C3	73(1)	90(2)	40(1)	-5(1)	21(1)	-15(1)
C4	57(1)	66(1)	46(1)	12(1)	14(1)	-8(1)
C5	42(1)	47(1)	45(1)	4(1)	15(1)	-3(1)
C6	44(1)	43(1)	40(1)	0(1)	16(1)	1(1)
C7	52(1)	36(1)	45(1)	0(1)	20(1)	3(1)
C8	49(1)	35(1)	44(1)	-1(1)	18(1)	1(1)
C9	64(1)	36(1)	58(1)	-2(1)	27(1)	-2(1)
C10	53(1)	38(1)	45(1)	-5(1)	19(1)	-2(1)
C11	50(1)	41(1)	42(1)	-5(1)	18(1)	-2(1)
C12	47(1)	47(1)	49(1)	-9(1)	23(1)	-7(1)
C13	45(1)	43(1)	48(1)	-10(1)	19(1)	-6(1)
C14	46(1)	44(1)	49(1)	-8(1)	20(1)	-1(1)
C15	44(1)	49(1)	53(1)	-6(1)	22(1)	-6(1)
C16	47(1)	42(1)	44(1)	-6(1)	16(1)	-7(1)
C17	73(1)	55(1)	94(2)	-14(1)	41(1)	-21(1)
C19	55(1)	55(1)	74(1)	-14(1)	28(1)	-15(1)
O1	102(1)	38(1)	58(1)	6(1)	40(1)	12(1)
O2	76(1)	41(1)	57(1)	11(1)	27(1)	9(1)
O3	70(1)	52(1)	75(1)	-22(1)	37(1)	-23(1)
O4	61(1)	54(1)	81(1)	-30(1)	39(1)	-20(1)
O5	65(1)	56(1)	80(1)	-24(1)	45(1)	-11(1)

The anisotropic displacement factor exponent takes the form:$-2\pi^2[\, h^2 a^{*2} U_{11} + ... + 2\, h\, k\, a^*\, b^*\, U_{12}\,]$

Table 2.3.4

Hydrogen coordinates (x 10^4) and isotropic displacement parameters
(Å^2 x 10^3)

Atom	x	y	z	$U_{(eq)}$
H18A	7800	-126	3473	128
H18B	7378	1117	2872	128
H18C	7467	-1086	2778	128
H18D	7090	1449	2642	118
H18E	7231	-657	2483	118
H18F	7692	411	3107	118
H1	5582	8615	6338	69
H2	5647	8267	7414	85
H3	5956	5355	7952	82
H4	6170	2761	7421	70
H9A	5416	2313	5376	62
H9B	6034	1479	5368	62
H10	6283	5899	4702	54
H12	5758	1168	4277	55
H15	7473	2667	3808	57
H17A	7807	7277	4494	106
H17B	7519	6066	3843	106
H17C	8034	5167	4468	106
H19A	5255	-3024	3333	91
H19B	5124	-807	3316	91
H19C	5447	-1859	3996	91

Table 2.3.5

Selected Bond lengths [Å] and angles [°] involving non- hydrogen atom with (e s d) in parentheses

Atoms	Bond Angles	Atoms	Bond Angles
C18A-O5	1.391(1)	C6-C5-C4	120.19(1)
C18B-O5	1.51(2)	C5-C6-C1	119.14(1)
C1-C2	1.378(3)	C5-C6-C7	120.42(3)
C1-C6	1.402(2)	C1-C6-C7	120.10(1)
C2-C3	1.388(3)	O1-C7-C6	121.91(1)
C3-C4	1.375(3)	O1-C7-C8	122.86(3)
C4-C5	1.399(2)	C6-C7-C8	115.15(2)
C5-O2	1.365(2)	C10-C8-C7	118.01(3)
C5-C6	1.394(2)	C10-C8-C9	127.13(3)
C6-C7	1.472(2)	C7-C8-C9	114.72(3)
C7-O1	1.2250(1)	O2-C9-C8	111.85(3)
C7-C8	1.484(2)	C8-C10-C11	130.25(1)
C8-C10	1.340(2)	C16-C11-C12	118.06(3)
C8-C9	1.502(2)	C16-C11-C10	118.00(1)
C9-O2	1.450(2)	C12-C11-C10	123.79(1)
C10-C11	1.456(2)	C13-C12-C11	121.55(1)
C11-C16	1.402(2)	O4-C13-C12	125.60(1)
C11-C12	1.408(2)	O4-C13-C14	115.39(3)
C12-C13	1.380(2)	C12-C13-C14	118.97(3)
C13-O4	1.3659(1)	O5-C14-C15	124.30(1)
C13-C14	1.406(2)	O5-C14-C13	115.24(3)
C14-O5	1.3619(1)	C15-C14-C13	120.44(3)
C14-C15	1.382(2)	C14-C15-C16	120.10(1)
C15-C16	1.385(2)	O3-C16-C15	123.64(2)
C16-O3	1.3653(1)	O3-C16-C11	115.51(3)
C17-O3	1.406(2)	C15-C16-C11	120.85(3)
C19-O4	1.412(2)	C5-O2-C9	115.26(2)
C2-C1-C6	120.59(1)	C16-O3-C17	119.17(2)
C1-C2-C3	119.34(1)	C13-O4-C19	117.97(2)
C4-C3-C2	121.45(1)	C14-O5-C18A	117.3(2)
C3-C4-C5	119.24(1)	C14-O5-C18B	117.3(1)
O2-C5-C6	122.62(3)	O2-C5-C4	117.15(1)

Table 2.3.6

Torsion angles [°] with (e s d) in parentheses

Atoms	Torsion angles	Atoms	Torsion angles
C6-C1-C2-C3	1.5(1)	C12-C11-C16-O3	-179.89(1)
C1-C2-C3-C4	-1.1(1)	C10-C11-C16-O3	4.4(2)
C2-C3-C4-C5	-0.6(1)	C12-C11-C16-C15	-0.4(2)
C3-C4-C5-O2	179.56(2)	C10-C11-C16-C15	-176.15(1)
C3-C4-C5-C6	1.9(1)	C6-C5-O2-C9	-22.8(2)
O2-C5-C6-C1	-179.02(2)	C4-C5-O2-C9	159.63(1)
C4-C5-C6-C1	-1.5(2)	C8-C9-O2-C5	48.94(1)
O2-C5-C6-C7	-5.7(2)	C15-C16-O3-C17	11.2(1)
C4-C5-C6-C7	171.77(2)	C11-C16-O3-C17	-169.37(1)
C2-C1-C6-C5	-0.2(1)	C12-C13-O4-C19	9.4(1)
C2-C1-C6-C7	-173.53(1)	C14-C13-O4-C19	-168.58(1)
C5-C6-C7-O1	-170.92(2)	C15-C14-O5-C18A	1.4(1)
C1-C6-C7-O1	2.3(1)	C13-C14-O5-C18A	179.7(2)
C5-C6-C7-C8	5.8(2)	C15-C14-O5-C18B	-24.6(2)
C1-C6-C7-C8	179.03(1)	C13-C14-O5-C18B	153.8(1)
O1-C7-C8-C10	21.9(2)	C12-C13-C14-C15	1.3(2)
C6-C7-C8-C10	-154.82(1)	O5-C14-C15-C16	176.39(1)
O1-C7-C8-C9	-162.17(1)	C13-C14-C15-C16	-1.9(2)
C6-C7-C8-C9	21.15(1)	C14-C15-C16-O3	-179.11(1)
C10-C8-C9-O2	127.42(1)	C14-C15-C16-C11	1.5(2)
C7-C8-C9-O2	-48.11(2)	O4-C13-C14-C15	179.38(1)
C7-C8-C10-C11	178.87(1)		
C9-C8-C10-C11	3.5(1)		
C8-C10-C11-C16	-145.92(1)		
C8-C10-C11-C12	38.6(1)		

Table 2.3.7

Least-square planes through the various groups of atoms and deviations (Å) for the compound.
Equation of the plane: $m1x + m2y + m3z = d$ where m1, m2, and m3 are direction cosines. *Starred

atoms are included in the plane calculations.

plane	m_1	m_2	m_3	D	Atom	Deviation (Å)
1	-0.9226	-0.1865	-0.3376	-12.9148	C7 *	-0.0272(1)
					C6 *	0. 0998(2)
					C5 *	-0.0100(2)
					C9*	0.3824(2)
					C8*	-0.1377(1)
					O2	-0.1224(1)
2	-0.2959	0.4863	-0. 8221	-9.6465	C16*	0.0031(1)
					C11*	0.0018(1)
					C12*	-0.0030(2)
					C13*	-0.0021(2)
					C14*	0.0080(2)
					C15*	-0.0090(1)
					O3	0.0054(1)

Table 2.3.8

Dihedral angle (°) formed by LSQ- planes for the compound
with (e s d) in parentheses

Plane- Plane	Angle (°)
1-2	62.6

Table 2.3.9

Hydrogen bonds geometry [Å and °]

D-H...A	D-H	H...A	D...A	D-H A
C4-H4...O5 #1	0.93	2.51	3.373(2)	154
C9-H9A...O1 #2	0.97	2.58	3.527(2)	165

Symmetry Code= #1   1-x,1-y,1-z ;   #2x,-y,1/2+z

Table 2.3.10

Geometry of the non- bonded Interaction [Å, °]

D-H...A	d(D-H)	d(H...A)	d(D...A)	<(DHA)
C(10)-H(10)...O1	0.93	2.45	2.814(2)	103

Table 2.3.11

Various contact contributions (%) in Hirshfeld surface

Inter contacts	Percentage (%)	Ratio (%)	Nature of Structure
ALL	100		
C-C	51.0	C-O/O-O=13.25	unknown
C-O/O-C	42.4		herringbone
O-O	3.2		

Table 2.4.1

Crystal data and structure refinement details (TMDB)

Crystal Data	TMDB	
Empirical formula	$C_{19}H_{18}O_5$	
Formula weight	326.33	
Temperature (K)	298(2)	
Wavelength (Å)	0.71073	
Crystal system	Monoclinic	
Space group	$P2_1/c$	
Unit cell dimensions (Å,°)	a = 15.200(1)	γ =94.357(2)
	b = 7.866(3)	
	c = 13.698(1)	
Volume ($Å^3$)	1633.1(1)	
Z	4	
Density (calculated) (Mg/m^3)	1.327	
Absorption coefficient (mm^{-1})	0.096	
F(000)	688	
Crystal size (mm)	0.300 x 0.250 x 0.200	
Theta range for data collection (°)	2.918 to 24.994	
Index ranges	$-18 \leq h \leq 18, -9 \leq k \leq 9, -16 \leq l \leq 16$	
Reflections collected	23685	
Independent reflections	2871 [R(int) = 0.0723]	
Completeness to theta = 24.994°	99.7 %	
Refinement method	Full-matrix least-squares on F^2	
Data / restraints / parameters	2871 / 0 / 220	
Goodness-of-fit on F^2	1.007	
Final R indices [I>2sigma(I)]	R1 = 0.061, wR2 = 0.172	
R indices (all data)	R1 = 0.092, wR2 = 0.211	
Extinction coefficient	n/a	
Largest diff. peak and hole ($e.Å^{-3}$)	0.38 and -0.32	

Table 2.4.2

Atomic coordinates $(x10^4)$ and equivalent isotropic displacement parameters $(Å^2 x 10^3)$ for non- hydrogen atom with (e s d) in parentheses

Atom	x	y	z	$U_{(eq)}$
O1	8535(1)	7075(3)	4316(2)	58(1)
O2	9260(1)	7198(3)	6248(2)	61(1)
O3	6632(2)	4688(1)	1721(2)	71(1)
O4	8917(2)	4768(3)	7506(2)	68(1)
O5	4873(1)	4331(3)	3804(2)	69(1)
C16	8320(2)	5856(1)	4979(2)	49(1)
C15	8692(2)	5912(1)	5933(2)	50(1)
C7	6125(2)	4374(1)	2352(2)	51(1)
C5	5175(2)	4095(1)	2110(2)	51(1)
C8	6422(2)	4274(2)	3410(2)	49(1)
C14	8511(2)	4617(1)	6589(2)	52(1)
C10	7252(2)	4683(1)	3695(2)	52(1)
C11	7689(2)	4618(1)	4683(2)	51(1)
C6	4836(2)	3904(1)	1142(3)	65(1)
C4	4592(2)	4138(2)	2839(2)	55(1)
C12	7529(2)	3340(1)	5352(2)	58(1)
C9	5743(2)	3686(1)	4076(2)	59(1)
C13	7944(2)	3315(1)	6285(2)	57(1)
C17	9431(2)	6969(2)	4050(3)	77(1)
C19	8714(3)	3521(1)	8218(3)	79(1)
C3	3690(2)	4040(1)	2608(3)	76(1)
C1	3948(3)	3776(1)	907(3)	80(1)
C2	3379(3)	3859(1)	1646(4)	83(1)
C18	8843(3)	8802(1)	6349(3)	87(1)

$U_{(eq)} = 1/3 \ \Sigma_i\Sigma_j \ U_{ij}a_i^* \ a_j^* \ a_ia_j$

Table 2.4.3

Anisotropic displacement parameters ($Å^2 x 10^3$) for non-hydrogen atoms

with (e s d) in parentheses

Atom	U_{11}	U_{22}	U_{33}	U_{23}	U_{13}	U_{12}
O1	41(1)	63(1)	69(1)	15(1)	0(1)	0(1)
O2	48(1)	60(1)	74(2)	-1(1)	-6(1)	-8(1)
O3	56(1)	102(2)	55(1)	4(1)	9(1)	3(1)
O4	61(1)	81(2)	59(1)	8(1)	-7(1)	-10(1)
O5	45(1)	98(2)	66(2)	-16(1)	10(1)	2(1)
C16	35(1)	50(2)	60(2)	5(1)	4(1)	5(1)
C15	33(1)	55(2)	63(2)	1(1)	2(1)	2(1)
C7	49(2)	52(2)	53(2)	-5(1)	6(1)	5(1)
C5	51(2)	43(2)	59(2)	-6(1)	0(1)	4(1)
C8	45(2)	50(2)	53(2)	-4(1)	4(1)	2(1)
C14	39(2)	59(2)	56(2)	-1(1)	1(1)	4(1)
C10	47(2)	56(2)	54(2)	1(1)	6(1)	2(1)
C11	40(2)	55(2)	58(2)	0(1)	4(1)	1(1)
C6	69(2)	62(2)	62(2)	-7(2)	-6(2)	3(2)
C4	48(2)	53(2)	64(2)	-9(2)	2(1)	-3(1)
C12	50(2)	56(2)	68(2)	-1(2)	0(2)	-5(1)
C9	50(2)	73(2)	55(2)	-2(2)	5(1)	-6(2)
C13	50(2)	56(2)	63(2)	11(2)	1(2)	0(1)
C17	50(2)	101(3)	82(2)	25(2)	12(2)	-1(2)
C19	71(2)	96(3)	67(2)	25(2)	-11(2)	-9(2)
C3	47(2)	80(2)	101(3)	-11(2)	5(2)	-3(2)
C1	80(3)	71(2)	85(3)	-8(2)	-30(2)	-3(2)
C2	56(2)	73(2)	117(4)	-8(2)	-25(2)	-7(2)
C18	86(3)	69(2)	103(3)	-21(2)	-3(2)	2(2)

The anisotropic displacement factor exponent takes the form:

$$-2\pi^2[h^2 a^{*2} U_{11} + ... + 2 h k a^* b^* U_{12}]$$

Table 2.4.4

Hydrogen coordinates (x 10^4) and isotropic displacement parameters
(Å^2x 10^3)

Atom	x	y	z	$U_{(eq)}$
H3	7597	5057	3205	62
H5	5221	3863	646	78
H7	7131	2481	5165	70
H1	5724	2454	4071	71
H2	5920	4046	4739	71
H9	7842	2423	6708	68
H4	9825	7290	4600	116
H6	9509	7723	3512	116
H8	9556	5825	3861	116
H10	8088	3482	8265	118
H11	9001	3819	8843	118
H12	8919	2427	8022	118
H13	3300	4095	3099	91
H14	3730	3635	260	96
H15	2774	3790	1489	100
H16	8635	9219	5715	130
H17	9259	9593	6654	130
H18	8354	8676	6747	130

Table 2.4.5

Selected Bond lengths [Å] and angles [°] involving non- hydrogen atom with (e s d) in parentheses

Atoms	Bond distances (Å)	Atoms	Bond angles (°)	Atoms	Bond angles (°)
O1-C16	1.377(1)	C16-O1-C17	113.8(2)	C16-C11-C10	119.7(1)
O1-C17	1.439(1)	C15-O2-C18	114.1(2)	C1-C6-C5	121.2(1)
O2-C15	1.377(1)	C14-O4-C19	117.6(1)	O5-C4-C5	122.0(1)
O2-C18	1.424(1)	C4-O5-C9	115.2(2)	O5-C4-C3	117.3(2)
O3-C7	1.227(1)	O1-C16-C15	120.0(1)	C5-C4 -C3	120.7(1)
O4-C14	1.362(1)	O1-C16-C11	118.8(1)	C13-C12-C11	121.9(1)
O4-C19	1.432 (1)	C15-C16-C11	121.1(1)	O5-C9-C8	113.3(1)
O5-C4	1.366(1)	O2-C15-C16	121.3(1)	C12-C13-C14	119.9(1)
O5-C9	1.439(1)	O2-C15-C14	118.9(1)	C2-C3-C4	119.2(1)
C16-C15	1.384(1)	C16-C15-C14	119.8(1)	C6-C1-C2	119.1(1)
C16-C11	1.405(1)	O3-C7-C5	121.9(1)	C1-C2-C3	121.3(2)
C15-C14	1.399(1)	O3-C7-C8	122.5(1)	C13-C14-C15	119.7(1)
C7-C5	1.473(1)	C5-C7-C8	115.6(2)	C8 -C10-C11	128.1(1)
C7-C8	1.487 (1)	C4-C5 -C6	118.6(2)	C12 -C11 - C16	117.3(2)
C5-C4	1.386(1)	C4-C5 -C7	120.3(2)	C12 -C11 -C10	128.1(2)
C5-C6	1.394(1)	C6-C5 -C7	121.0(2)	O4-C14-C15	115.6(2)
C8-C10	1.332(1)	C10- C8-C7	118.9(1)	C12-C11-C10	123.0(2)
C8-C9	1.501 (1)	C10-C8-C9	125.2(1)	C8-C10-C11	128.1(2)
C14-C13	1.383(1)	C7-C8-C9	115.9(2)	C12-C11- C16	117.3(1)
C10-C11	1.462 (1)	O4-C14 -C13	124.8(1)	C16 - C11-C10	119.7(1)
C11-C12	1.394(1)	C13 -C14 -C15	119.7(1)		
C6-C1	1.368(2)				
C4-C3	1.386(1)				
C12-C13	1.382(1)				
C3-C2	1.373(1)				
C1-C2	1.382(1)				

Table 2.4.6

Torsion angles [°] with (e s d) in parentheses

Atoms	Torsion angles	Atoms	Torsion angles
C17-O1-C16-C15	68.7(1)	O2-C15-C14-O4	0.8(1)
C17-O1-C16-C11	-114.4(2)	C16-C15-C14-O4	179.1(2)
C18-O2-C15-C16	71.7(1)	O2-C15-C14-C13	-179.9(2)
C18-O2-C15-C14	-110.1(2)	C16-C15-C14-C13	-1.7(1)
O1-C16-C15-O2	1.9(1)	C7-C8-C10-C11	-177.6(2)
C11-C16-C15-O2	-175.0(2)	C9-C8-C10-C11	1.7(1)
O1-C16-C15-C14	-176.4(2)	O1-C16-C11-C12	176.0(1)
C11-C16-C15-C14	6.8(1)	C15-C16-C11-C12	-7.1(1)
O3-C7-C5-C4	-164.9(1)	O1-C16-C11-C10	-2.2(1)
C8-C7-C5-C4	14.3(1)	C15-C16-C11-C10	174.6(1)
O3-C7-C5-C6	10.5(2)	C8-C10-C11-C12	37.2(1)
C8-C7-C5-C6	-170.4(1)	C8-C10-C11-C16	-144.6(1)
O3-C7-C8-C10	5.9(1)	C4-C5-C6-C1	0.5(1)
C5-C7-C8-C10	-173.2(2)	C7-C5-C6-C1	-174.9(2)
O3-C7-C8-C9	-173.4(2)	C9-O5-C4-C5	-28.7(1)
C5-C7-C8-C9	7.5(1)	C9-O5-C4-C3	153.3(2)
C19-O4-C14-C13	-2.5(1)	C6-C5-C4-O5	-179.6(2)
C19-O4-C14-C15	176.7(2)	C4-C3-C2-C1	-0.1(1)
C7-C5-C4-O5	-4.1(1)	O5-C4-C3-C2	179.5(2)
C6-C5-C4-C3	-1.7(1)	C5-C4-C3-C2	1.5(1)
C7-C5-C4-C3	173.8(2)	C5-C6-C1-C2	0.8(1)
C16-C11-C12-C13	2.5(1)	C6-C1-C2-C3	-1.0(1)
C10-C11-C12-C13	-179.4(2)		
C4-O5-C9-C8	49.3(1)		
C10-C8-C9-O5	142.4(1)		
C7-C8-C9-O5	-38.3(1)		
C11-C12-C13-C14	2.5(2)		
O4-C14-C13-C12	176.3(1)		
C15-C14-C13-C12	-2.9(1)		

Table 2.4.7

Least-square planes through the various groups of atoms and deviations (Å) for the compound.

Equation of the plane: $m_1x + m_2y + m_3z = d$ where m_1, m_2, and m_3 are direction cosines.

*Starred atoms are included in the plane calculations.

plane	m_1	m_2	m_3	D	Atom	Deviation (Å)
1	0.1443	-0.9989	-0.0426	-3.3485	C4 *	0.0278(1)
					C5 *	0. 1184(2)
					C7 *	-0.0945(2)
					C8*	-0.0725(2)
					C9*	0.3343(1)
					C10	-0.3931(2)
					O5	-0.1751(1)
2	0.7794	- 0.5454	-0. 3080	-4.8076	C13*	0.0288(1)
					C12*	0.0061(1)
					C11*	-0.0283(2)
					C16*	0.0395(2)
					C15*	-0.0224(2)
					C14*	-0.0103(1)
					O1	0.1034(1)

Table 2.4.8

Dihedral angle (°) formed by LSQ- planes for the compound with (e s d)

in parentheses

Plane-Plane	Angle (°)
1-2	55.3

Table 2.4.9

Hydrogen bonds geometry [Å and °]

D-H...A	d(D-H)	d(H...A)	d(D...A)	<(DHA)
C13-H9...O3 #1	0.93	2.48	3.177(4)	132
C17-H6...O4 #2	0.96	2.53	3.380(5)	147
C2-H15...O1 #3	0.93	2.58	3.404(5)	148

Symmetry Code =#1x,3/2-y,-1/2+z #2 -x+1,-1/2+y,-1/2-z #3 x,1/2-y,1/2+z

Table 2.4.10

Geometry of the non- bonded Interaction [Å,°]

D-H...A	d(D-H)	d(H...A)	d(D...A)	<(DHA)
C10-H3...O3	0.93	2.43	2.795(4)	103
C17-H15...O2	0.96	2.48	3.047(5)	118
C18-H21...O1	0.96	2.55	3.102(4)	117

Table 2.4.11

Various contact contributions (%) in Hirshfeld surface

Inter contacts	Percentage (%)	Ratio (%)	Nature of Structure
ALL	100		
H-H	51.0		
H-O/O-H	24.4		Herringbone structure
H-C/C-H	17.5	C-H/C-C = 3.57	
C-C	4.9		
O-C/C-O	2.2		

Table 2.5.1

Crystal data and structure refinement details (DFDB)

Crystal Data	DFDB	
Empirical formula	$C_{16}H_{10}F_2O_2$	
Formula weight	272.24	
Temperature (K)	296(2)	
Wavelength (Å)	0.71073	
Crystal system	Monoclinic	
Space group	Cc	
Unit cell dimensions (Å,°)	a =23.629(2)	β=91.038(1)
	b =3.9354(3)	
	c = 13.4340(1)	
Volume ($Å^3$)	1249.01(2)	
Z	4	
Density (calculated) (Mg/m^3)	1.448	
Absorption coefficient (mm^{-1})	0.115	
F(000)	560	
Crystal size (mm)	0.200 x 0.200 x 0.150	
Theta range for data collection (°)	3.033 to 25.308	
Index ranges	$-28 \leq h \leq 28, -4 \leq k \leq 4, -16 \leq l \leq 16$	
Reflections collected	10262	
Independent reflections	2276 [R(int) = 0.0392]	
Completeness to theta = 25.242°	99.9 %	
Refinement method	Full-matrix least-squares on F^2	
Data / restraints / parameters	2276 / 0 / 182	
Goodness-of-fit on F^2	0.956	
Final R indices [I>2sigma(I)]	R1 = 0.047, wR2 = 0.126	
R indices (all data)	R1 = 0.054, wR2 = 0.159	
Absolute structure parameter	-0.4(4)	
Extinction coefficient	0.000(3)	
Largest diff. peak and hole (e.Å^{-3})	0.16 and -0.10	

Table 2.5.2

Atomic coordinates (x10^4) and equivalent isotropic displacement parameters

(Å^{2}x 10^3) for non- hydrogen atom with (e s d) in parentheses

Atom	x	y	z	U$_{(eq)}$
F1	3528(1)	3866(1)	4427(2)	92(1)
F2	2806(1)	3429(2)	5916(3)	103(1)
O2	6014(2)	3657(1)	5289(3)	79(1)
C12	3692(2)	5134(2)	5324(3)	65(1)
C7	5464(2)	6978(2)	3636(1)	65(1)
C13	3318(2)	4906(3)	6095(1)	72(1)
C11	4230(2)	6474(1)	5449(3)	60(1)
C10	4602(2)	6694(1)	4606(3)	64(1)
C8	5168(2)	6475(1)	4596(3)	62(1)
C3	6315(2)	4435(1)	4458(1)	66(1)
C2	6067(2)	6017(1)	3637(3)	62(1)
C16	4363(2)	7717(1)	6405(3)	68(1)
C14	3462(2)	6056(3)	7025(1)	77(1)
C1	6397(2)	6540(3)	2792(1)	75(1)
C15	3986(2)	7498(3)	7164(3)	74(1)
C9	5542(2)	5784(2)	5497(1)	70(1)
C4	6880(2)	3454(3)	4444(1)	82(2)
C6	6953(2)	5536(1)	2785(1)	88(2)
C5	7191(2)	4008(1)	3615(2)	90(2)
O1	5218(2)	8043(2)	2894(3)	89(1)

U$_{(eq)}$ = 1/3 $\Sigma_i\Sigma_j$U$_{ij}$a$_i$* a$_j$* a$_i$a$_j$

Table 2.5.3

Anisotropic displacement parameters (Å^2 x 10^3) for non-hydrogen atoms
with (e s d) in parentheses

Atom	U_{11}	U_{22}	U_{33}	U_{23}	U_{13}	U_{12}
F1	66(2)	141(3)	67(2)	-11(2)	-19(1)	-9(2)
F2	59(2)	154(3)	97(2)	8(2)	-7(2)	-11(2)
O2	71(2)	80(2)	86(2)	22(2)	-15(2)	9(2)
C12	59(2)	77(3)	57(2)	2(2)	-14(2)	10(2)
C7	66(3)	65(2)	64(3)	7(2)	-12(2)	-7(2)
C13	51(2)	86(3)	77(3)	11(2)	-12(2)	9(2)
C11	60(2)	61(2)	58(2)	4(2)	-14(2)	4(2)
C10	69(3)	62(2)	61(2)	5(2)	-16(2)	1(2)
C8	62(2)	59(2)	65(3)	7(2)	-18(2)	-5(2)
C3	62(2)	62(2)	74(3)	0(2)	-13(2)	-2(2)
C2	58(2)	58(2)	68(3)	-3(2)	-12(2)	-9(2)
C16	70(3)	60(2)	72(3)	1(2)	-17(2)	-1(2)
C14	73(3)	87(3)	70(3)	7(2)	-2(2)	14(2)
C1	75(3)	79(3)	71(3)	-8(2)	-6(2)	-12(2)
C15	93(3)	72(3)	56(2)	-7(2)	-12(2)	10(2)
C9	63(2)	79(3)	68(3)	10(2)	-15(2)	-2(2)
C4	74(3)	78(3)	94(4)	-2(3)	-20(3)	7(3)
C6	70(3)	102(4)	91(4)	-14(3)	5(3)	-6(3)
C5	64(3)	89(3)	116(5)	-22(3)	-8(3)	6(3)
O1	71(2)	126(3)	68(2)	26(2)	-14(2)	1(2)

The anisotropic displacement factor exponent takes the form:

$$-2\pi^2[\,h^2 a^{*2} U_{11} + ... + 2\,h\,k\,a^*\,b^*\,U_{12}\,]$$

Table 2.5.4

Hydrogen coordinates $(\times 10^4)$ and isotropic displacement parameters $(\text{Å}^2 \times 10^3)$

Atom	x	y	z	$U_{(eq)}$
H10	4425	7034	3990	77
H16	4715	8711	6524	81
H14	3212	5867	7550	92
H1	6238	7578	2232	90
H15	4088	8346	7788	89
H9A	5680	7931	5761	84
H9B	5317	4715	6006	84
H4	7045	2419	4999	99
H6	7168	5885	2222	105
H5	7568	3346	3609	96

Table 2.5.5

Selected Bond lengths [Å] and angles [°] involving non- hydrogen

atom with (e s d) in parentheses

Atoms	Bond distance (Å)	Atoms	Bond angle (°)	Atoms	Bond angle (°)
F1-C12	1.356(1)	F1-C12-C13	117.9(1)	C15-C16-C11	121.4(1)
F2-C13	1.360(1)	F1-C12-C11	119.7(1)	C13-C14-C15	118.1(1)
O2-C3	1.369(1)	C13-C12-C11	122.3(1)	C6-C1-C2	120.7(1)
O2-C9	1.427(1)	O1-C7-C8	121.9(1)	C14-C15-C16	121.5(1)
C12-C13	1.377(1)	O1-C7-C2	122.4(2)	O2-C9-C8	113.4(1)
C12-C11	1.383(1)	C8-C7-C2	115.7(1)	C5-C4-C3	119.9(1)
C7-O1	1.220(1)	F2-C13-C14	120.7(1)	C5-C6-C1	119.8(1)
C7-C8	1.491(2)	F2-C13-C12	118.4(1)	C4-C5-C6	120.8(1)
C7-C2	1.473(1)	C14-C13-C12	120.9(1)		
C13-C14	1.366(2)	C12-C11-C16	115.7(1)		
C11-C16	1.404(2)	C12-C11-C10	119.8(2)		
C11-C10	1.451(2)	C16-C11-C10	124.3(2)		
C10-C8	1.340(2)	C8-C10-C11	128.4(2)		
C8-C9	1.510(1)	C10-C8-C7	118.9(1)		
C3-C4	1.389(2)	C10-C8-C9	124.9(1)		
C3-C2	1.387(1)	C7-C8-C9	116.1(1)		
C2-C1	1.405(2)	O2-C3-C4	117.5(1)		
C16-C15	1.368(2)	O2-C3-C2	122.0(1)		
C14-C15	1.372(2)	C4-C3-C2	120.4(1)		
C1-C6	1.370(2)	C3-C2-C1	118.3(1)		
C4-C5	1.363(2)	C3-C2-C7	120.7(1)		
C6-C5	1.377(2)	C1-C2-C7	120.9(1)		

Table 2.5.6

Torsion angles [°] with (e s d) in parentheses

Angles	Torsion angles	Angles	Torsion angles
F1-C12-C13-F2	0.0(2)	C7-C2-C1-C6	-177.8(1)
C11-C12-C13-F2	-177.4(1)	C13-C14-C15-C16	-1.6(2)
F1-C12-C13-C14	178.3(1)	C11-C16-C15-C14	0.0(2)
C11-C12-C13-C14	1.0(2)	C3-O2-C9-C8	46.4(1)
F1-C12-C11-C16	-179.8(1)	C10-C8-C9-O2	142.4(1)
C13-C12-C11-C16	-2.5(2)	C7-C8-C9-O2	-38.3(1)
F1-C12-C11-C10	3.6(2)	O2-C3-C4-C5	176.6(1)
C13-C12-C11-C10	-179.1(1)	C2-C3-C4-C5	-0.8(2)
C12-C11-C10-C8	-148.6(1)	C2-C1-C6-C5	-0.2(2)
C16-C11-C10-C8	35.1(2)	C3-C4-C5-C6	0.0(2)
C11-C10-C8-C7	-176.6(1)	C1-C6-C5-C4	0.5(2)
C11-C10-C8-C9	2.7(2)	C3-C2-C1-C6	-0.6(2)
O1-C7-C8-C10	10.4(2)	C8-C7-C2-C1	-176.7(1)
C2-C7-C8-C10	-167.9(1)	C12-C11-C16-C15	2.0(2)
O1-C7-C8-C9	-168.9(1)	C10-C11-C16-C15	178.5(1)
C2-C7-C8-C9	12.8(2)	F2-C13-C14-C15	179.5(1)
C9-O2-C3-C4	154.1(1)	C12-C13-C14-C15	1.1(2)
C9-O2-C3-C2	-28.5(1)	O1-C7-C2-C1	5.0(2)
O2-C3-C2-C1	-176.2(1)		
C4-C3-C2-C1	1.1(2)		
O2-C3-C2-C7	1.0(2)		
C4-C3-C2-C7	178.2(1)		
O1-C7-C2-C3	-172.1(1)		
C8-C7-C2-C3	6.2(2)		

Table 2.5.7

Least-square planes through the various groups of atoms and deviations (Å) for the compound.
Equation of the plane: m1x + m2y + m3z =d where m1, m2, and m3 are direction cosines.

*Starred atoms are included in the plane calculations

plane	m_1	m_2	m_3	D	Atom	Deviation (Å)
1	-0.3371	-0.9027	-0.2670	-8.1481	C2*	-0.0973(1)
					C3*	-0. 0209(2)
					C7 *	0.0418(2)
					C8*	0.1200(2)
					C9*	-0.2481(1)
					C10	0.4893(2)
					O2	0.2046(1)
2	-0.3615	0.8996	-0. 2449	-3.0514	C11*	-0.0146(1)
					C12*	0.0107 (1)
					C13*	0.0024(2)
					C14*	-0.0114(2)
					C15*	0.0070(2)
					C16*	0.0059(1)
					F2	-0.0254(1)

Table 2.5.8

Dihedral angle (°) formed by LSQ- planes for the compound

with (e s d) in parentheses

Plane-Plane	Angle (°)
1-2	51.3

Table 2.5.9

Hydrogen bonds geometry [Å and °]

D-H...A	d(D-H)	d(H...A)	d(D...A)	<(DHA)
C9-H9A...O2 #1	0.97	2.47	3.307(6)	144
C16-H16...O1 #2	0.93	2.52	3.274(6)	138

Symmetry Code = #1 x, 1+y, z   #2 x,2-y,1/2+z

Table 2.5.10

Geometry of the non- bonded Interaction [Å, °]

D-H...A	d(D-H)	d(H...A)	d(D...A)	<(DHA)
C10-H10...O1	0.93	2.44	2.794(6)	103

Table 2.5.11

Various contact contributions (%) in Hirshfeld surface

Inter contacts	Percentage (%)	Ratio (%)	Nature of Structure
ALL	100		
C-C	35.3		
C-F	19.7		β structure
F-C	15.1	C-F/C-C=2.75	
C-O	14.1		
F-F	1.7		
O-O	1.4		

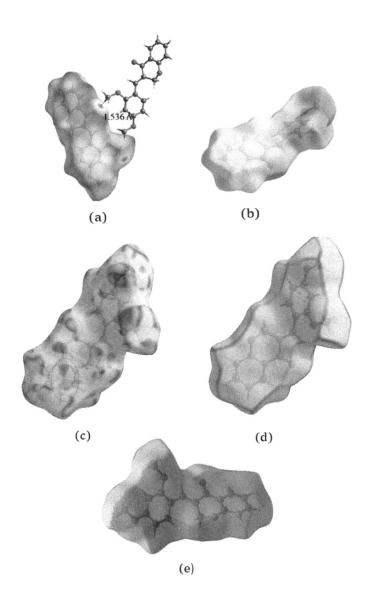

(a)

(b)

(c)

(d)

(e)

FIG. 2.4. HIRSHFELD SURFACE MAPPED OVER (a) dnorm (b) ELECTROSTATIC POTENTIAL (c) SHAPE INDEX (d) CURVEDNESS (e) FRAGMENT PATCHES (DBDB)

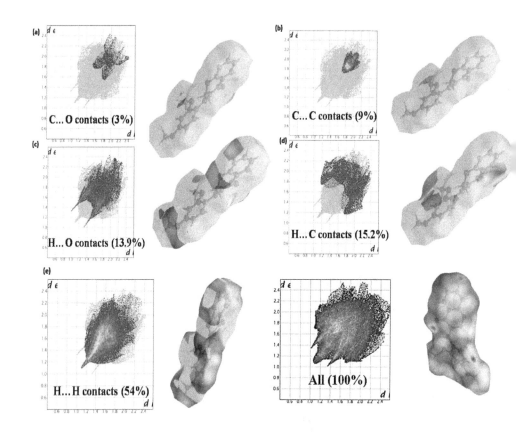

FIG.2.5. TWO-DIMENSIONAL FINGERPRINT PLOT FOR THE TITLE COMPOUND SHOWING THE DELINEATED CONTRIBUTIONS: (a) C-O CONTACTS, (b) C-C CONTACTS, (c) H-O CONTACTS, (d) H -C CONTACTS, (e) H-H CONTACTS AND THE WHOLE (DBDB)

Table 2.6. Interaction energies (kJ mol^{-1}) calculated with scaling factor

Color	N	Sym. op	Electron Density	R	E_{elec}	E_{pol}	E_{disp}	E_{rep}	E_{total}
	2	x+1/2,- y+1/2, -z	B3LYP/631G (d,p)	4.00	-9.2	-4.7	-83.6	43.0	-59.3
	2	-x+1/2,-y,-z+1/2	B3LYP/631G (d,p)	9.44	-6.7	-2.2	-21.0	12.6	-19.2
	2	-x+1/2,-y,-z+1/2	B3LYP/631G (d,p)	10.38	-4.2	-2.6	-15.2	9.7	-13.6
	2	x,y,z	B3LYP/631G (d,p)	13.41	-5.8	-0.8	-9.5	4.9	-12.0
	2	-x+1/2,y+1/2,-z+1/2	B3LYP/631G (d,p)	9.79	-12.1	-4.5	-14.3	12.5	-20.8
	2	-x+1/2,y+1/2,-z+1/2	B3LYP/631G (d,p)	9.79	-2.1	-0.5	-16.7	9.0	-11.6
	2	-x,-y,-z	B3LYP/631G (d,p)	13.31	-0.4	-0.2	-4.0	0.5	-3.8
Energy Model					K_ele	K_pol	K_disp		K_rep
CE-B3LYP … B3LYP/6-31G (d,p) electron densities					1.057	0.740	0.871		0.618

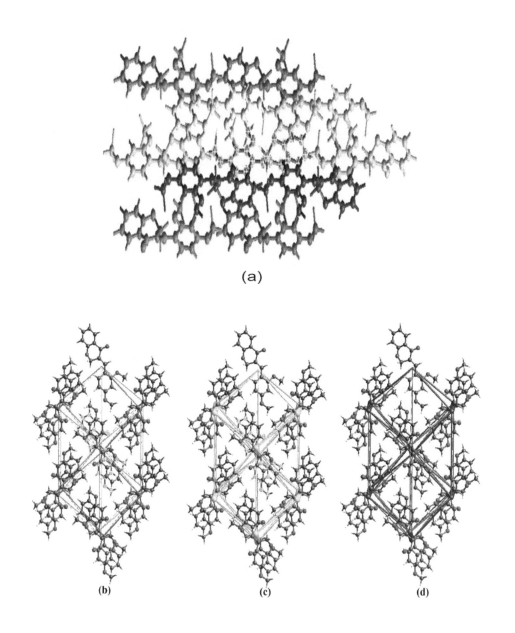

(a)

(b)   (c)   (d)

FIG. 2.6. (a) INTERACTION BETWEEN THE SELECTED MOLECULE AND THE MOLECULES
AROUND 3.8 Å RADIUS (b) ELECTROSTATIC ENERGY (c) DISPERSION ENERGY AND (d)
TOTAL ENERGY (DBDB)

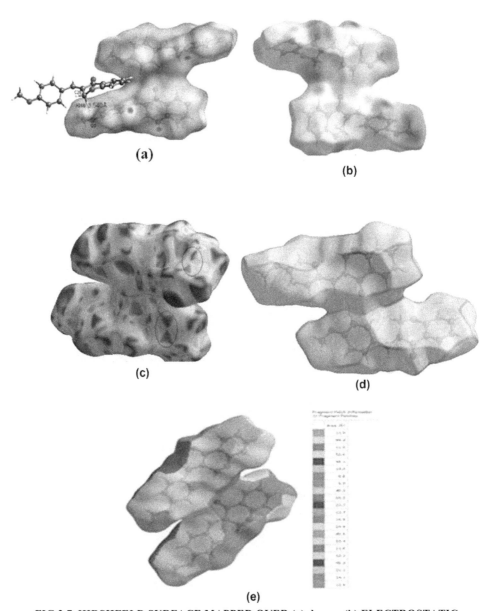

FIG.2.7. HIRSHFELD SURFACE MAPPED OVER (a) dnorm (b) ELECTROSTATIC POTENTIAL (c) SHAPE INDEX (d) CURVEDNESS (e) FRAGMENT PATCHES FOR THE COMPOUND MPDB

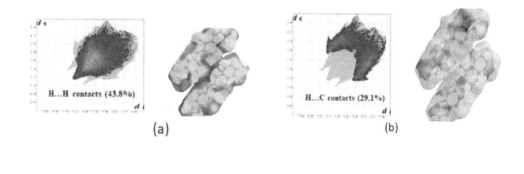

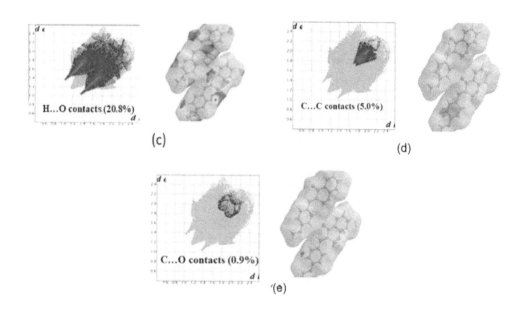

FIG.2.8. 2D-FINGER PRINT PLOT OF MPDB SHOWING (a) H-H CONTACTS (b) H-C CONTACTS (c) H-O CONTACTS (d) C-C CONTACTS (e) O-C CONTACTS

Table 2.7. The interaction energies (kJ mol^{-1}) calculated with scaling factor

Color	N	Sym. op	Electron Density	R	E_{pol}	E_{elec}	E_{disp}	E_{rep}	E_{total}
	1	-x, -y, -z	B3LYP/631G (d,p)	5.29	-3.0	-11.2	-49.0	21.0	-43.8
	2	x,y,z	B3LYP/631G (d,p)	16.81	-0.6	0.6	-6.5	4.5	-2.7
	2	x,y,z	B3LYP/631G (d,p)	7.64	-2.1	-5.1	-20.2	12.6	-16.6
	1	-	B3LYP/631G (d,p)	8.10	0.0	0.0	-0.0	0.0	0.0
	1	-x,-y,-z	B3LYP/631G (d,p)	5.53	-1.8	-8.2	-41.6	21.9	-32.7
	1	-x,-y,-z	B3LYP/631G (d,p)	15.19	-0.4	-1.0	-4.6	1.0	-4.8
	2	x, y, z	B3LYP/631G (d,p)	12.52	-1.2	-6.6	-10.8	.6.3	-13.5
	1	-	B3LYP/631G (d,p)	6.87	-2.1	-5.1	-20.2	12.6	-16.6
	1	-x, -y, -z	B3LYP/631G (d,p)	13.71	-0.4	-3.4	-11.0	7.5	-8.8
	1	-	B3LYP/631G (d,p)	8.09	-1.2	-6.6	-10.8	6.3	-13.5
	1	-	B3LYP/631G (d,p)	9.69	-0.6	0.6	-6.5	4.5	-2.7

Energy Model			K_ele	K_pol		K_disp	K_rep	
CE-B3LYP ... B3LYP/6-31G (d,p) electron densities			1.057	0.740		0.871	0.618	

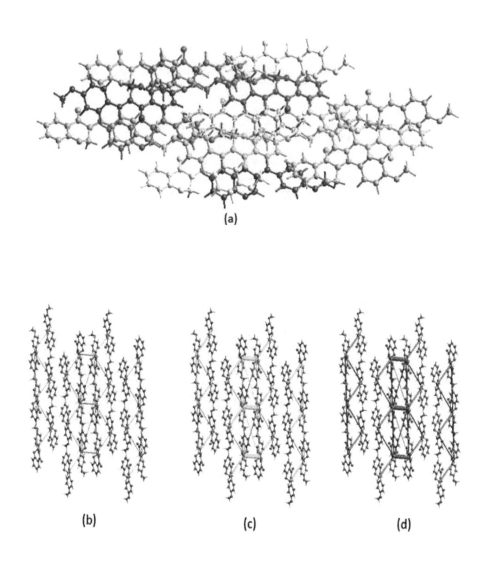

(a)

(b)   (c)   (d)

FIG.2.9. (a) INTERACTION BETWEEN THE SELECTED MOLECULE AND THE MOLECULES AROUND 3.8 Å RADIUS (b) ELECTROSTATIC ENERGY (c) DISPERSION ENERGY AND (d) TOTAL ENERGY (MPDB)

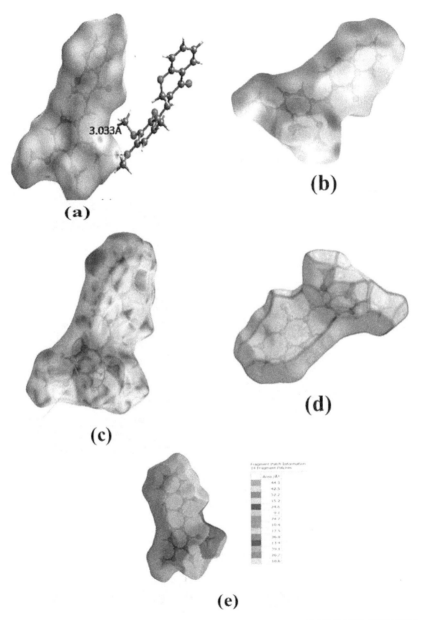

FIG.2.10. HIRSHFELD SURFACE MAPPED OVER (a) dnorm (b) ELECTROSTATIC POTENTIAL (c) SHAPE INDEX (d) CURVEDNESS (e) FRAGMENT PATCHES FOR THE COMPOUND TPDB

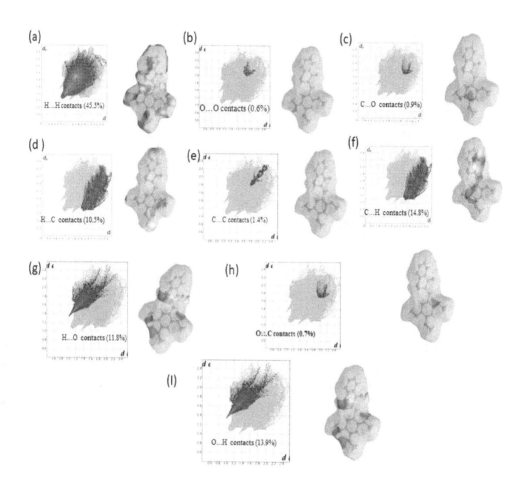

FIG.2.11. 2D-FINGER PRINT PLOT OF TPDB SHOWING (a) H-H CONTACTS (b) O-O CONTACTS (c) C-O CONTACTS (d) H-C CONTACTS (e) C-C CONTACTS (f) C-H CONTACTS (g) H-O CONTACTS (h) O-CCONTACTS (i) O-H CONTACTS

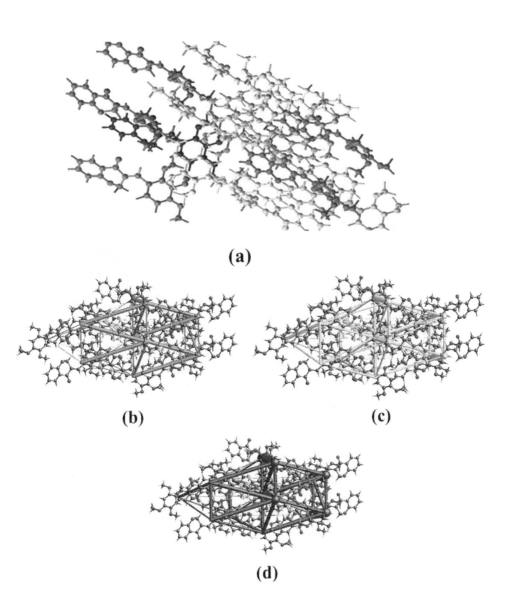

(a)

(b)

(c)

(d)

FIG.2.12. (a) INTERACTION BETWEEN THE SELECTED MOLECULE AND THE
MOLECULES AROUND 3.8 Å RADIUS (b) ELECTROSTATIC ENERGY (c) DISPERSION
ENERGY AND (d) TOTAL ENERGY (TPDB)

Table 2.8. The interaction energies (kJ mol^{-1}) calculated with scaling factor

Color	N	Sym. op	Electron Density	R	E_{elec}	E_{pol}	E_{disp}	E_{rep}	E_{total}
	2	-x+1/2, y+1/2,z+1/2	B3LYP/631G (d,p)	13.82	-31.3	-8.4	-15.7	25.1	-37.4
	2	x,-y,z+1/2	B3LYP/631G (d,p)	11.78	-3.1	-3.4	-19.6	18.7	-11.3
	1	-x,-y,-z	B3LYP/631G (d,p)	7.95	-6.6	-1.7	-27.7	17.0	-21.9
	2	x,y,z	B3LYP/631G (d,p)	6.94	-12.7	-8.7	-38.0	23.4	-38.5
	1	-x+1/2,-y+1/2,-z	B3LYP/631G (d,p)	5.25	-34.4	-19.8	-88.6	52.5	-95.7
	1	-x, y, -z+1/2	B3LYP/631G (d,p)	9.90	-3.8	-0.3	-5.3	0.3	-8.7
	2	x,-y,z+1/2	B3LYP/631G (d,p)	11.22	-8.3	-2.0	-29.8	16.8	-25.8
	1	-x,-y, -z	B3LYP/631G (d,p)	7.09	-13.3	-5.1	-45.0	28.8	-39.3
	1	-x,y,-z+1/2	B3LYP/631G (d,p)	15.11	-0.3	-0.2	-5.4	0.7	-4.7
	1	-x+1/2,-y+1/2,-z	B3LYP/631G (d,p)	7.92	-26.0	-5.5	-25.8	15.2	-44.2
Energy Model				K_ele		K_pol		K_disp	K_rep
CE-B3LYP ... B3LYP/6-31G (d,p) electron densities				1.057		0.740		0.871	0.618

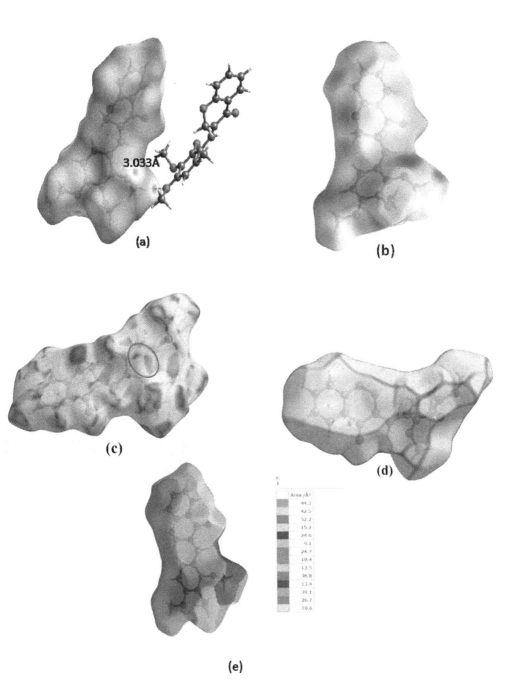

FIG.2.13. HIRSHFELD SURFACE MAPPED OVER (a) dnorm (b) ELECTROSTATIC POTENTIAL (c) SHAPE INDEX (d) CURVEDNESS (e) FRAGMENT PATCHES FOR THE COMPOUND TMDB

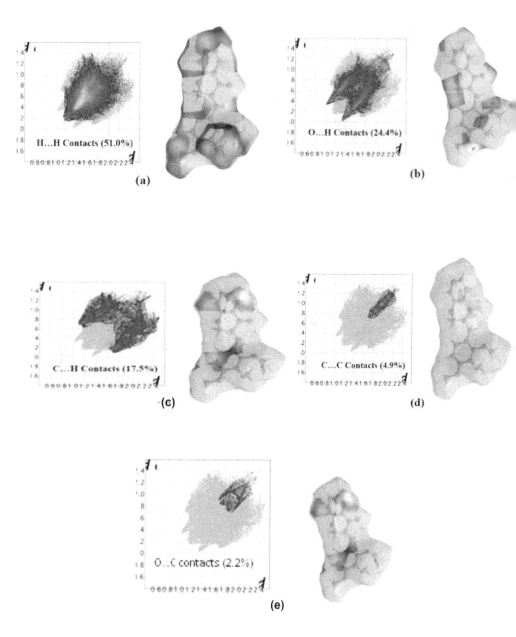

FIG.2.14. 2D-FINGER PRINT PLOT OF TMDB SHOWING (a) H-H CONTACTS (b) O-H CONTACTS (c) C-H CONTACTS (d) C-C CONTACTS (e) O-C CONTACTS

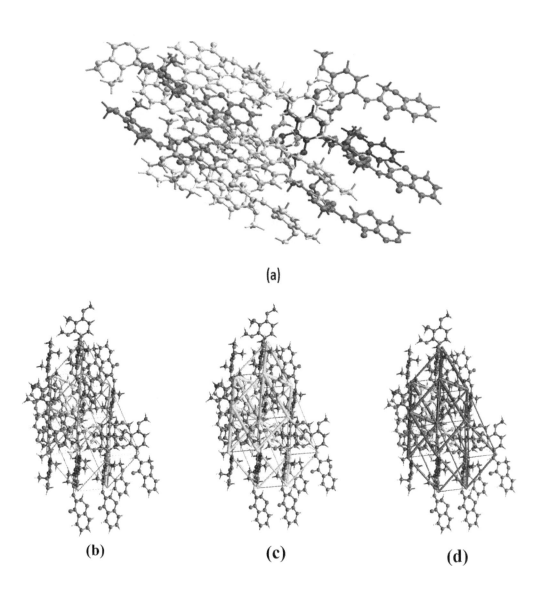

FIG.2.15. (a) INTERACTION BETWEEN THE SELECTED MOLECULE AND THE MOLECULES AROUND 3.8 Å RADIUS (b) ELECTROSTATIC ENERGY (c) DISPERSION ENERGY AND (d) TOTAL ENERGY (TMDB)

Table 2.9. The interaction energies (kJ mol^{-1}) calculated with scaling factor

Color	N	Sym. op	Electron Density	R	E_{pol}	E_{elec}	E_{disp}	E_{rep}	E_{total}
	2	-x, y+1/2, -z+1/2	B3LYP/631G (d,p)	8.33	-2.5	-7.5	-47.2	26.0	-34.9
	2	x,-y+1/2,z+1/2	B3LYP/631G (d,p)	7.81	-4.3	-11.4	-34.0	24.7	-29.5
	2	x,y,z	B3LYP/631G (d,p)	7.87	-0.5	1.4	-9.1	2.0	-5.6
	1	-x,-y,-z	B3LYP/631G (d,p)	12.68	-2.0	-7.3	-13.9	9.8	-15.3
	2	x,-y+1/2,z+1/2	B3LYP/631G (d,p)	7.99	-3.6	-7.9	-21.8	13.6	-21.5
	1	-x, -y, -z	B3LYP/631G (d,p)	6.39	-2.3	-13.7	-47.0	30.8	-38.2
	1	-x, -y, -z	B3LYP/631G (d,p)	9.36	-1.0	-5.0	-27.9	11.6	-23.2
	2	-x,-y+1/2, -z+1/2	B3LYP/631G (d,p)	12.96	-1.5	-5.5	-11.5	5.7	-13.4
	1	-x, -y, -z	B3LYP/631G (d,p)	12.34	-0.2	1.1	-6.1	1.8	-3.1
Energy Model					K_ele		K_pol		K_disp	K_rep
CE-B3LYP ... B3LYP/6-31G (d,p) electron densities					1.057		0.740		0.871	0.618

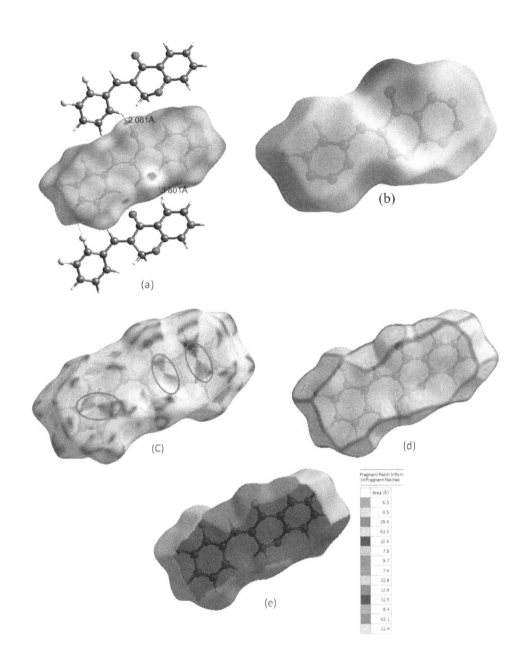

FIG.2.16. HIRSHFELD SURFACE MAPPED OVER (a) dnorm (b) ELECTROSTATIC POTENTIAL (c) SHAPE INDEX (d) CURVEDNESS (e) FRAGMENT PATCHES FOR THE COMPOUND DFDB

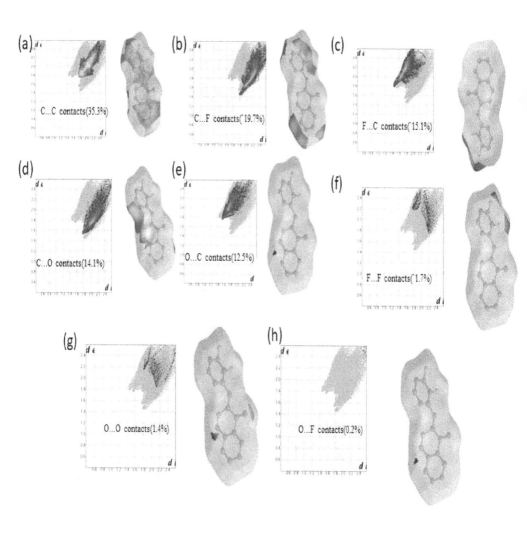

(a) C...C contacts(35.3%)

(b) C...F contacts(19.7%)

(c) F...C contacts(15.1%)

(d) C...O contacts(14.1%)

(e) O...C contacts(12.5%)

(f) F...F contacts(1.7%)

(g) O...O contacts(1.4%)

(h) O...F contacts(0.2%)

FIG.2.17. 2D-FINGER PRINT PLOT OF DFDB SHOWING (a) C-C CONTACTS (b) C-F CONTACTS (c) F-C CONTACTS (d) C-O CONTACTS (e) O-C CONTACTS (f) F-F CONTACTS (g) O-O CONTACTS (h) O-F CONTACTS

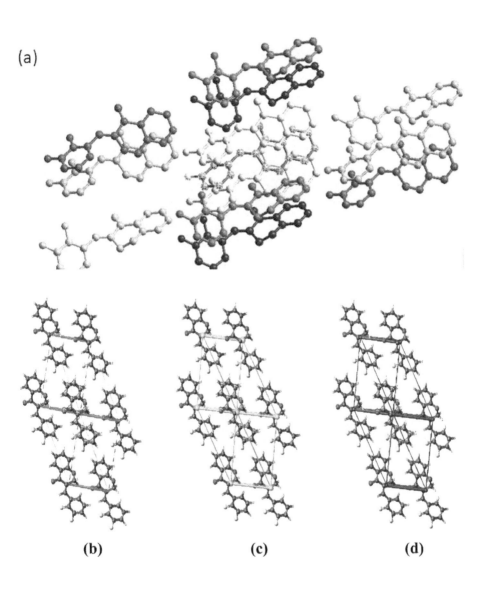

**FIG.2.18. (a) INTERACTION BETWEEN THE SELECTED MOLECULE AND THE
MOLECULES AROUND 3.8 Å RADIUS (b) ELECTROSTATIC ENERGY (c) DISPERSION
ENERGY AND (d) TOTAL ENERGY (DFDB)**

Table 2.10. The interaction energies (kJ mol^{-1}) calculated with scaling factor

Color	N	Sym. op	Electron Density	R	E_{pol}	E_{elec}	E_{disp}	E_{rep}	E_{total}
	2	x+1/2,y+1/2, z	B3LYP/631G (d,p)	11.98	-0.1	-0.6	-4.0	0.7	-3.8
	2	x,y,z	B3LYP/631G (d,p)	3.94	-2.0	2.8	-53.1	24.6	-29.6
	2	x+1/2,y+1/2, z	B3LYP/631G (d,p)	11.98	-0.2	-1.1	-3.9	0.7	-4.2
	2	x+1/2,-y+1/2, z+1/2	B3LYP/631G (d,p)	13.90	-0.2	-0.8	-2.8	0.4	-3.2
	2	x,-y, z+1/2	B3LYP/631G (d,p)	6.73	-1.0	-1.0	-14.3	.6.8	-10.1
	2	x,-y, z+1/2	B3LYP/631G (d,p)	7.58	-1.0	-0.6	-6.8	3.0	-5.5
Energy Model			K_ele		K_pol		K_disp		K_rep
3CE-B3LYP …B3LYP/6-31G (d,p) electron densities			1.057		0.740		0.871		0.618

CHAPTER-III

STUDY OF BIOLOGICAL ACTIVITIES OF THE SYNTHESIZED COMPOUND

3. INTRODUCTION

Flavonids consist of a massive group of polyphenolic compounds having a benzo-γ-pyrone structure and are ubiquitously found in plants. They are synthesized through a phenyl propanoid pathway. Available reviews exhibit that secondary metabolites of phenolic nature such a flavonoids are accountable for the range of pharmacological activities [130]. Flavonoids are hydroxylated phenolic elements and are recognized to be synthesized through flowers in response to microbial infection [131]. Their activities are structure dependent. The chemical nature of flavonoids depends on their structural class, degree of hydroxylation, different substitutions and conjugations, and degree of polymerization [132]. Recent activity in these materials has been encouraged via the potential health advantages arising from the antioxidant activities of these polyphenolic compounds. Functional hydroxyl agencies in flavonoids mediate their antioxidant results through scavenging free radicals and or via chelating metal ions [133]. Due to their high antioxidant content, flavonoids are thought to offer health promoting qualities as a dietary component capability in both in vivo and in vitro structures [134]. Flavonoids can induce human protecting enzyme systems. A variety of research has recommended shielding the effects of flavonoids from many infections (bacterial and viral diseases and degenerative illnesses such as cardiovascular diseases, cancers, and different age-related illness [135]. Flavonoids additionally act as a secondary antioxidant defense system in plant tissues exposed to different abiotic and biotic stresses. They additionally modify growth factors in flowers such as auxin. Flavonoids are additionally recognized to impact the great balance of foods via performing as flavorings, colorants, and antioxidants. Flavonoids contained in berries may also have a positive impact on Parkinson's disease and may also assist to enhance memory in elderly people. Intake of antioxidant flavonoids has been inversely associated with the danger of incidence of dementia.

3.1 MATERIALS AND METHODS
3.1.1 ANTIMICROBIAL ACTIVITY

The standard strains of Gram-positive bacteria: *Salmonella typhi* and *Micrococcus luteu,* Gram-negative bacteria species: *Staphylococcus aureus* and *Pseudomonas aeruginosa* and fungi species: *Candida albicans, Aspergillus niger, Trichoderma viride*, were used in the test. Stock solutions of the test compound and standard drug were diluted two-fold in the microplate wells. Solutions of the synthesized compounds were prepared at 500,750, and

1000µg/mL concentrations, and the standard drug was prepared at 1mg/mL concentration. During antibacterial susceptibility testing, 100 µL of Mueller Hinton Broth (MHB) was added to each well of the microplate, and the bacterial suspension of the bacteria at 10^5 CFU/mL concentrations was inoculated into the solutions of the compound. A 20 µL bacterial inoculum was added to each well of the microplates and is incubated at 37°C for 24 h. Then the antimicrobial activity was determined by measuring the diameter of the zone of inhibition [136]. Antifungal activity of the sample was determined by the disc diffusion method on Sabouraud Dextrose Agar (SDA) medium [137]. SDA medium is poured into the petriplate. After the medium was solidified, the inoculums were spread on the solid plates with a sterile swab moistened with the fungal suspension. Amphotericin-B is taken as a positive control. Samples and positive control of 20 µL each were added to sterile discs and placed in SDA plates. The plates were incubated at 28°C for 24h. Then antifungal activity was determined by measuring the diameter of the zone of inhibition.

3.1.2 ANTIOXIDANT ACTIVITY

The antiradical activity of the title compound was determined using the free radical, 1,1-Diphenyl-1-picrylhydrazyl (DPPH). In its radical form, DPPH has an absorption band at 520 nm which disappears upon reduction by an antiradical compound. Test tubes with 3.7 mL of absolute methanol in 100 µL of the sample and 200µL of DPPH solution at room temperature stirred for the 20sand were left in the dark [138]. The absorbance of the solutions at 517 nm was measured using a UV Spectrophotometer for which a mixed solution of 100µL of absolute methanol and 100µL of Butylated Hydroxytoluene (BHT) was used as the blank. The absorbance measured with the sample was expressed as, the absorbance at the addition of methanol replacing the sample as absorbance at the blank, and the (%)of antioxidant activity.

3.1.3 CYTOTOXICITY AND ANTICANCER ACTIVITY INVESTIGATION – MTT ASSAY

VERO cell lines (normal) and MCF-7 cell lines (cancerous) were obtained from the National Centre for Cell Sciences, Pune (NCCS). The cells were maintained in Gibco Dulbecco's Modified Eagle Medium (DMEM) supplemented with 10% FBS, penicillin (100 U/mL), and streptomycin (100 µg/mL) in a humidified atmosphere of 50 µg/mL CO_2 at 37°C. Cells (1×10^5/well) were plated in 24-well plates and incubated at 37°C with a 5% CO_2 condition. After the cell reaches the confluence, the various concentrations of the sample were added and incubated for 24h. After incubation, the sample was removed from the well and washed with phosphate-buffered saline (pH 7.4) or DMEM without serum. 100µL/well (5mg/mL) of 0.5% 3-(4,5-dimethyl-2-thiazolyl)-2,5-diphenyl-tetrazolium bromide (MTT) was added and incubated for 4h. After incubation, 1mL of DMSO was added to all the wells. The absorbance at 570nm was measured with a UV Spectrophotometer using DMSO as the blank. Measurements were performed and the concentration required for half minimal inhibition (IC_{50}) was determined graphically. The anticancer activity test of the synthesized chalcone analoge on MCF-7 breast carcinoma was also performed by MTT assay [139].

3.2 RESULTS AND DISCUSSION

3.2.1 ANTIBACTERIAL AND ANTIFUNGAL ACTIVITY STUDIES

The newly synthesized chromenone derivative was subjected to DBDB, MPDB, TPDB, TMDB, and DFDB antibacterial screening against two Gram-positive bacteria (*Salmonella typhi* and *Micrococccus luteu*) and the Gram-negative bacteria (*Staphylococcus aureus* and *Pseudomonas aeruginosa*) and three fungi species: *Candida albicans, Aspergillus niger, Trichoderma viride* by Agar disk diffusion method. The estimated zone of inhibition of the compound against Gram-positive and Gram-negative bacteria/fungi compared with the reference antibiotic drug Ampicillin (1mg/mL), were listed in Tables 3.1 & 3.2. The fungus *Aspergillus niger* have better activity than standard drug. For interpretation the results was also represented in Figures 3.1-3.4, respectively. The zone of inhibition recorded at various concentrations (500, 750 ,and 1000 µg/mL) of the title compound showed that the tested microorganisms for all the compounds show completely resistant to both antibacterial and antifungal activities and to the antibiotic. All the compounds had shown antibacterial activity, however, DBDB, MPDB, TPDB, and TMDB, showed moderate resistivity to the bacterial strains but DFDB shows comparable (to the reference drug molecule) antibacterial activity against both Gram positive and Gram negative bacterial strains. Whereas intermediate antifungal activity has been exhibited by all the synthesized compounds against the tested microorganisms. The fungus *Aspergillus niger* has demonstrated excellent and superior activity to the conventional medication.

3.2.2 ANTIOXIDANT ACTIVITY STUDY

The synthesized compounds DBDB, MPDB, TPDB, TMDB, and DFDB were subjected to its their antioxidant activity by the standard free radical scavenging DPPH assay method (Table 3.3 and Fig. 3.6). The o- and p-substitution by electron donating groups may increase the antioxidant activities of chalcone [140]. For the title compounds DBDB, MPDB, TPDB, TMDB, and DFDB, the percentage of DPPH inhibition which is the measure of the percentage of antioxidant activity was observed to be 48.7, 42.4, 42.1, 28.2, and 38.7%, respectively (Fig.3.5).Among the synthesized compounds, the chalcone derivative DBDB showed highest antioxidant activity. Overall, the antioxidant activities of all the compounds are significant (28.2-48.7%)

3.2.3 CYTOTOXIC EFFECT ON NORMAL VERO CELL LINE

The cytotoxic effect of the tested compounds DBDB, MPDB, TPDB, TMDB and DFDB on the normal VERO cell line was recorded by varying the sample concentration and quantifying the cell viability (Table 3.4). A graph relating the sample concentration and the cell viability (Fig.3.7) is extrapolated to calculate the IC_{50} (half maximal inhibitory concentration). It is noticed that as the concentration of the sample increases, the cell viability decreases slowly to 50% of its initial value at a half-maximal inhibitory concentration (IC_{50}) > 1000 μg/mL, thus indicating less toxicity (Fig.3.7, Table 3.4). Also, the morphological changes of Vero cells to the varying sample concentration were compared to untreated cells, which shows the decrease of normal cells as the sample concentration increases. The title compounds DBDB, MPDB, TPDB, TMDB and DFDB exhibits 60.51, 64.24, 61.88, 58.57 and 59.56%, cell viability at a high concentration of 1000 μg/mL. Indicative of IC_{50} at concentration > 1000 μg/mL, and thus the compounds are nontoxic to Vero cell line up to 1000 μg/mL (maximum testing concentration). The non-toxic effect of all the compounds tested for concentrations ranging from 1000 to 7.8 μg/mL. The surface morphology changes recorded at a concentration of 1000 and 7.8μg/mL (available limit) are shown in Fig. 3.8. Since IC_{50}>1000 μg/mL, all the synthesized compounds are observed to exhibit a low cytotoxic effect on the normal cell lines.

3.2.4 ANTICANCER ACTIVITY ON MCF-7 CELL LINES

The anticancer proliferative activity of the synthesized compounds DBDB, MPDB, TPDB, TMDB, and DFDB on MCF-7 cell lines was evaluated by using an MTT assay method, in which the cell viability is measured for various sample concentrations (Table 3.5). It is observed that the cell viability decreases as the concentration of the sample increases IC_{50} value of the compounds DBDB, MPDB, TPDB, TMDB, and DFDB is 7.8, 15.6, 31.2 and 15.6 μg/mL (Fig. 3.9 & Table 3.6), which demonstrate its efficacy as potential anti-cancer material in the field of drug designing. The recorded surface morphology changes of MCF-7 cells treated with the synthesized compounds at 1000 and 7.8μg/mL concentrations are shown in Fig. 3.10. The IC_{50} value corresponds to a lower sample concentration of about 7.8μg/mL clearly illustrating the high toxicity against cancerous cells, and thus the title molecules can be considered as a lead drug candidate to fight against breast cancer. All the compounds of DBDB, MPDB, TPDB, TMDB, and DFDB have shown significant anticancer activity even at lower concentrations of the samples (Fig. 3.11 & Table 3).

Table 3.1 Antibacterial activities of the compounds

Compounds	Microorganisms	Zone of Inhibition (mm) Concentration(µg/mL)			Antibiotic Ampicillin (1 mg/mL)
		1000	750	500	
DBDB	*Salmonella typhi*	8	7	-	13
	Micrococcus luteus	8	-	-	15
	Staphylococcus aureus	8	7	7	12
	Pseudomonas aeruginosa	8	7	-	10
MPDB	*Salmonella typhi*	8	7	-	11
	Micrococcus luteus	8	7	-	15
	Staphylococcus aureus	7	-	-	10
	Pseudomonas aeruginosa	8	-	-	10
TPDB	*Salmonella typhi*	8	7	7	10
	Micrococcus luteus	9	8	7	14
	Staphylococcus aureus	7	-	-	10
	Pseudomonas aeruginosa	8	8	7	10
TMDB	*Salmonella typhi*	9	8	7	10
	Micrococcus luteus	9	8	8	13
	Staphylococcus aureus	7	-	-	12
	Pseudomonas aeruginosa	8	-	-	10
DFDB	***Salmonella typhi***	**9**	**8**	**7**	**11**
	Micrococcus luteus	**9**	**8**	**8**	**15**
	Staphylococcus aureus	**9**	**8**	**8**	**10**
	Pseudomonas aeruginosa	**9**	**9**	**8**	**10**

Table 3.2 The antifungal activity of the compounds

Compounds	Microorganisms	Zone of Inhibition (mm)			Antibiotic Amphotericin B (1 mg/mL)
		Concentration (µg/mL)			
		1000	750	500	
DBDB	*Candida albicans*	8	8	7	15
	Aspergillus niger	8	7	7	7
	Trichoderma viride	10	9	-	21
MPDB	*Candida albicans*	8	8	7	17
	Aspergillus niger	10	9	7	7
	Trichoderma viride	8	8	7	17
TPDB	*Candida albicans*	7	7	7	16
	Aspergillus niger	8	8	7	8
	Trichoderma viride	9	8	-	16
TMDB	*Candida albicans*	7	-	-	16
	Aspergillus niger	8	8	7	8
	Trichoderma viride	-	-	-	16
DFDB	*Candida albicans*	-	-	-	13
	Aspergillus niger	9	9	9	10
	Trichoderma viride	8	8	9	10

Compounds	*Salmonella typhi*	*Micrococccus luteu*	*Staphylococcus aureus*	*pseudomonas aeruginosa*
DBDB	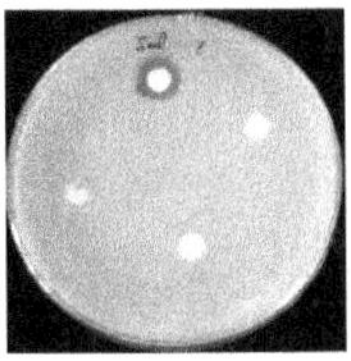	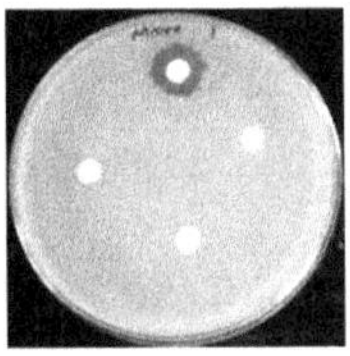	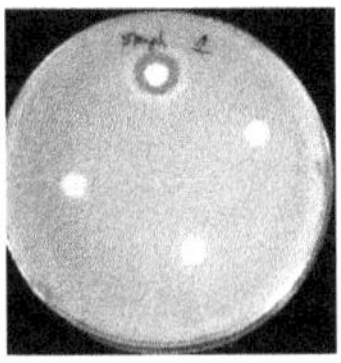	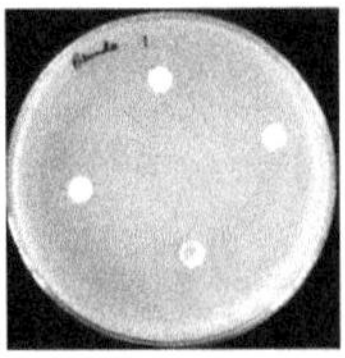
MPDB	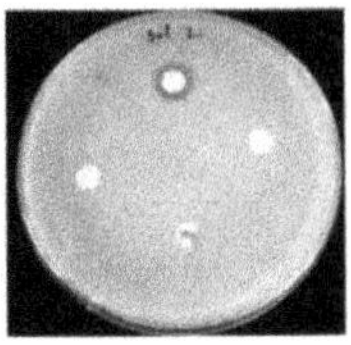	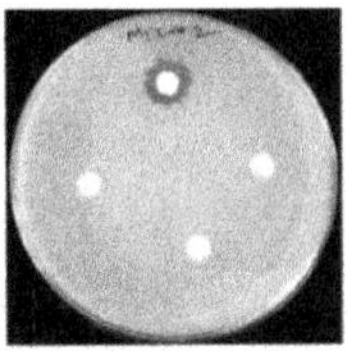	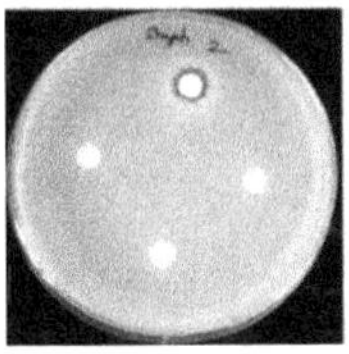	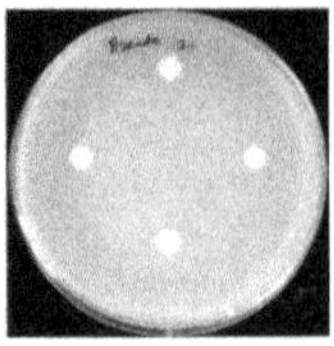
TPDB	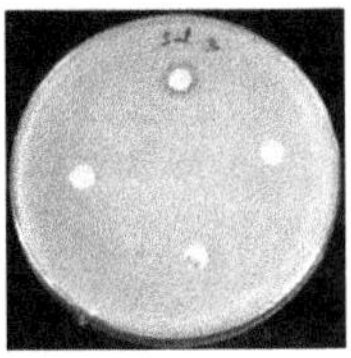	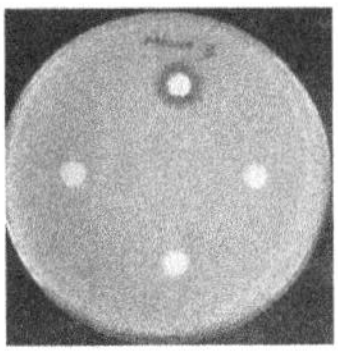	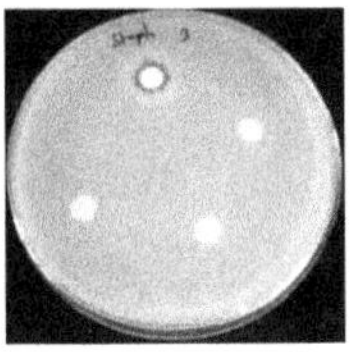	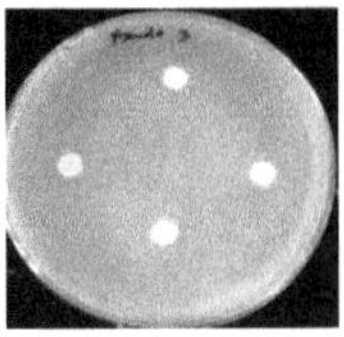
TMDB	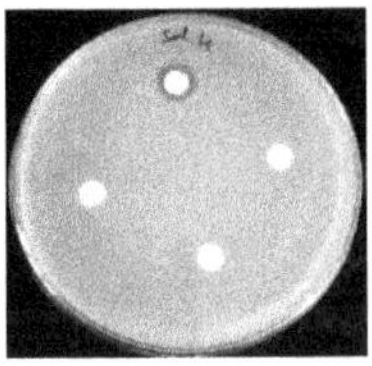	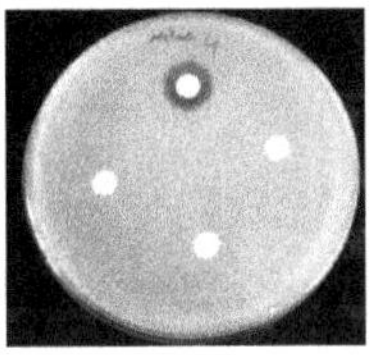	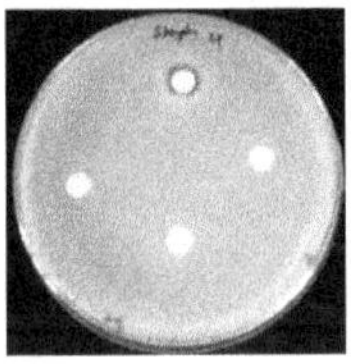	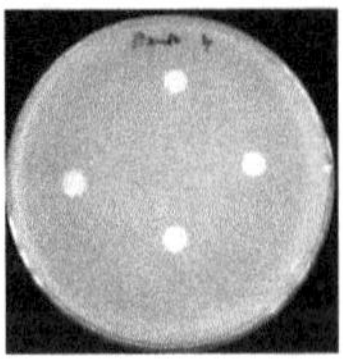
DFDB	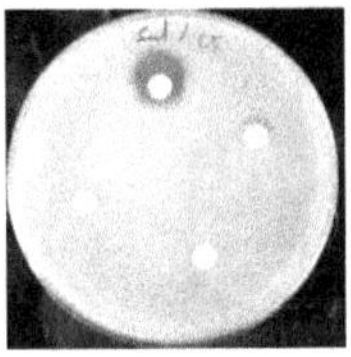	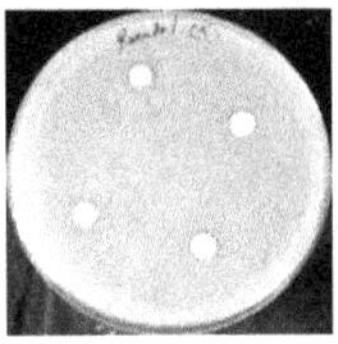	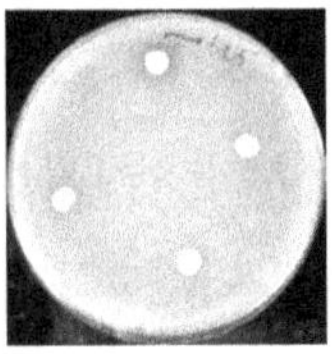	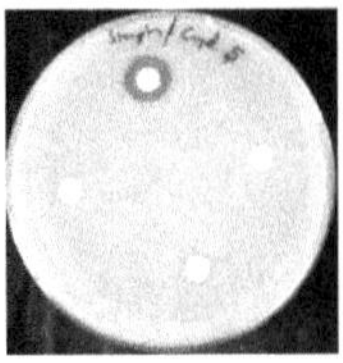

FIG.3.1. ANTIBACTERIAL ACTIVITIES OF ALL COMPOUNDS (ZONE OF INHIBITION)

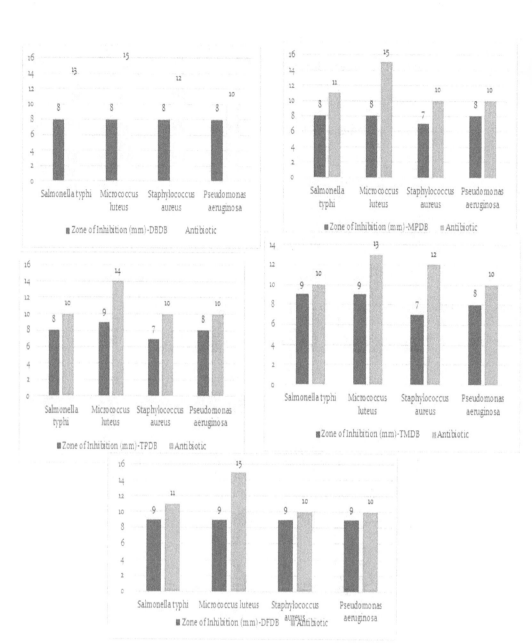

FIG. 3.2 ANTIBACTERIAL ACTIVITY OF COMPOUNDS DBDB, MPDB, TPDB, TMDB AND DFDB

Compounds	Candida albicans	Aspergillus niger	Trichoderma viride
DBDB			
MPDB			
TPDB			
TMDB			

| DFDB | 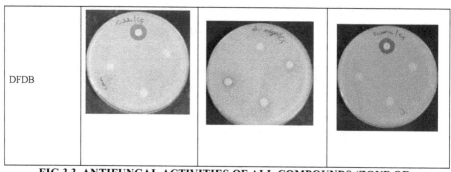 |

FIG.3.3. ANTIFUNGAL ACTIVITIES OF ALL COMPOUNDS (ZONE OF INHIBITION)

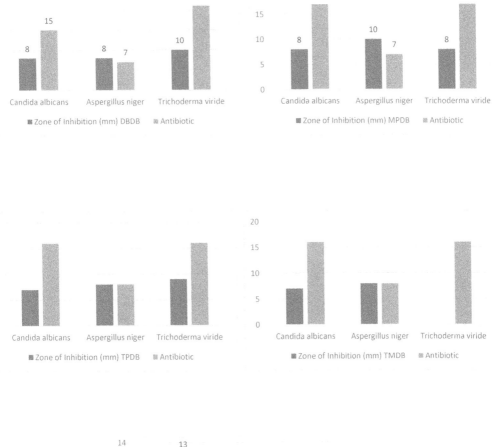

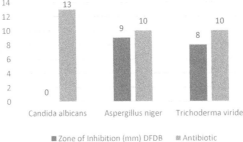

FIG. 3.4 ANTIFUNGAL ACTIVITY OF COMPOUNDS DBDB, MPDB, TPDB, TMDB AND DFDB

Table 3.3 Antioxidant activity of the compounds

Compounds	O.D Value	DPPH activity (%)
DBDB	0.15	48.7
MPDB	0.22	42.4
TPDB	0.22	42.1
TMDB	0.27	28.2
DFDB	0.23	38.7
Standard-BHT	0.002	99.7

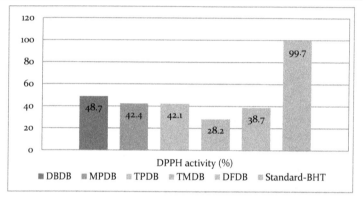

FIG. 3.5 ANTIOXIDANT ACTIVITY OF COMPOUNDS DBDB, MPDB, TPDB, TMDB AND DFDB

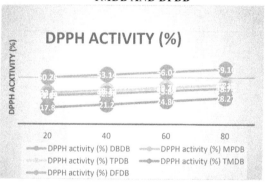

FIG. 3.6 IN-VITRO DPPH ACTIVITY OF ALL THE COMPOUNDS DBDB, MPDB, TPDB, TMDB AND DFDB

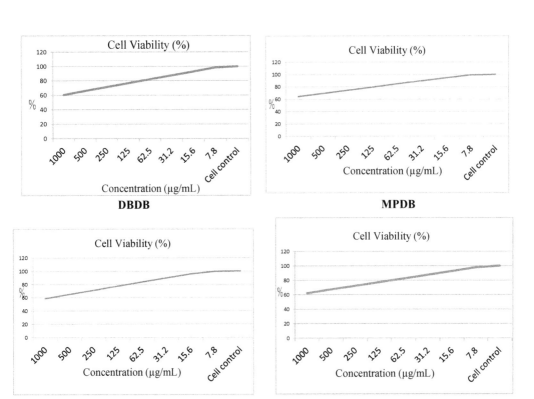

DBDB

MPDB

TPDB

TMDB

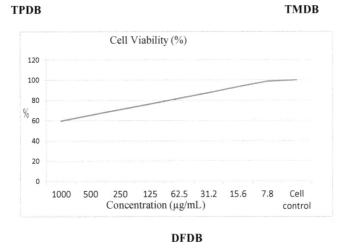

DFDB

FIG. 3.7 CYTOTOXIC ACTIVITY OF COMPOUNDS ON VERO CELL LINE

Compounds	Normal VERO Cell line	Sample at 1000μg/ mL	Sample at 7.8μg/mL
DBDB			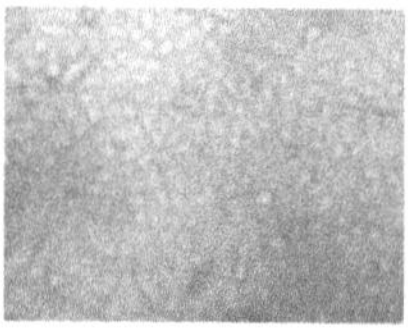
MPDB		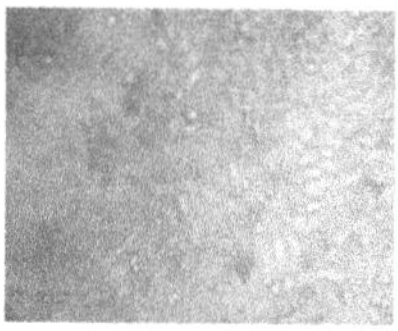	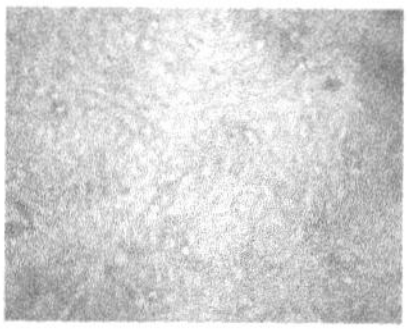
TPDB			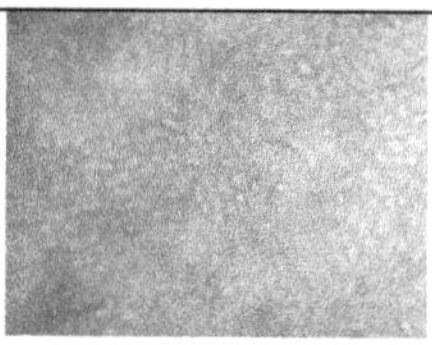
TMDB		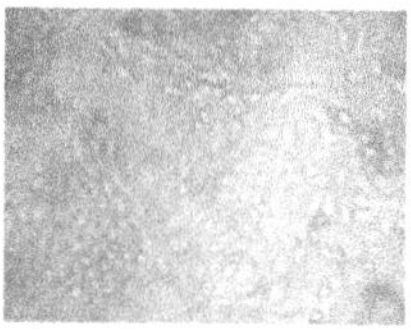	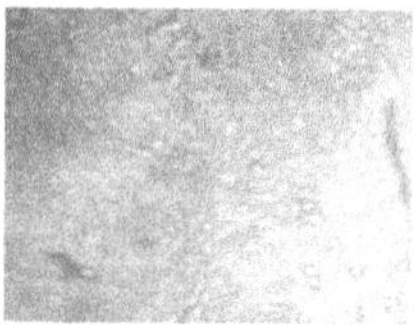
DFDB		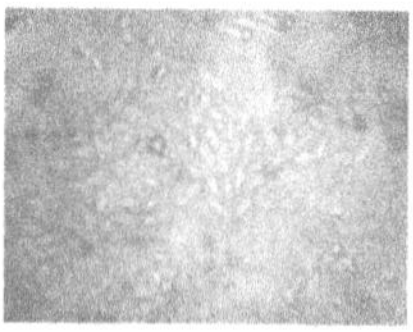	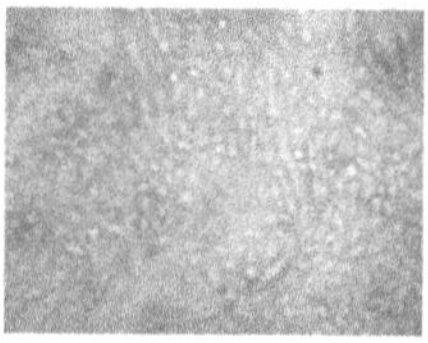

FIG.3.8. CYTOTOXIC EFFECT OF ALL COMPOUNDS

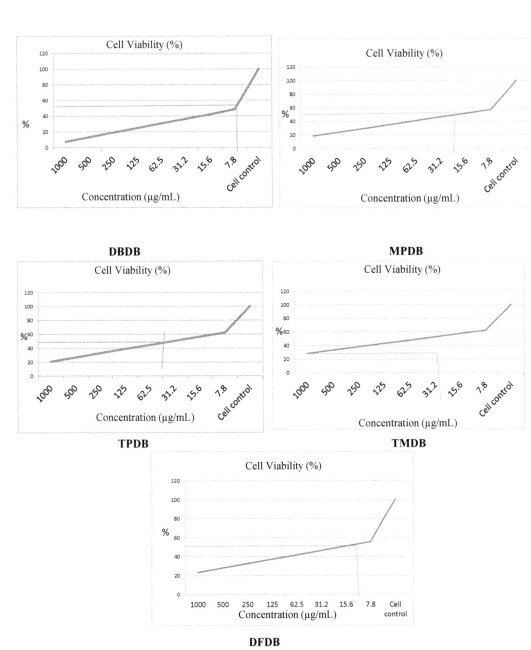

DBDB

MPDB

TPDB

TMDB

DFDB

FIG. 3.9 ANTICANCER ACTIVITY OF COMPOUNDS ON VERO CELL LINE

Compounds	Normal VERO Cell line	Sample at 1000 µg/mL	Sample at 7.8µg/mL
DBDB		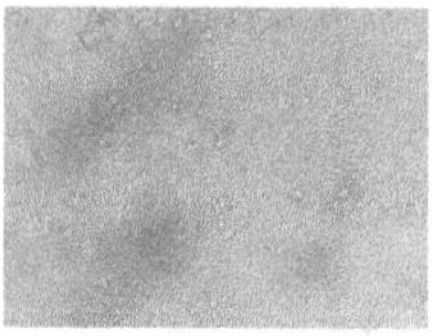	
MPDB			
TPDB			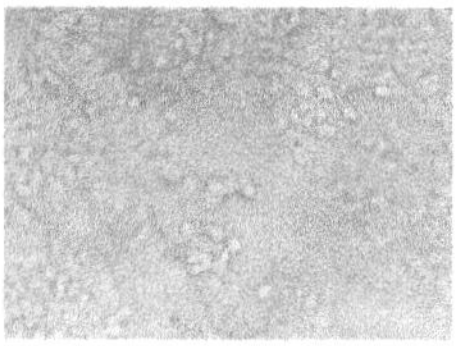
TMDB	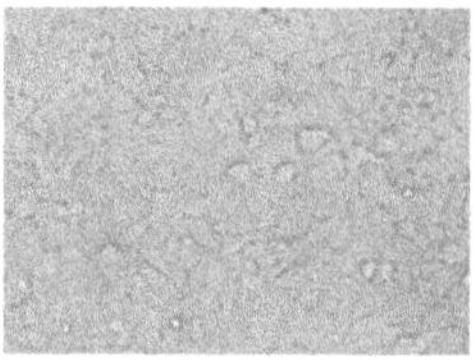	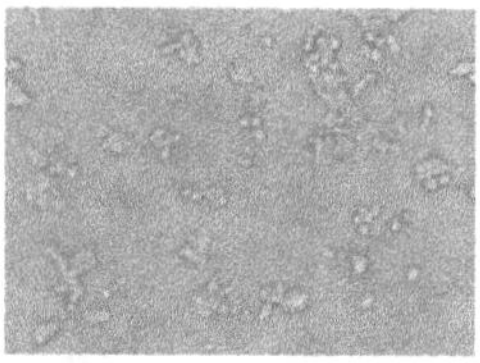	
DFDB			

FIG. 3.10. ANTICANCER ACTIVITIES OF ALL COMPOUNDS VIA SURFACE MORPHOLOGY CHANGES

Table 3.6 IC_{50} values of the compounds

Compounds	IC_{50} values
DBDB	7.8
MPDB	15.6
TPDB	31.2
TMDB	31.2
DFDB	15.6

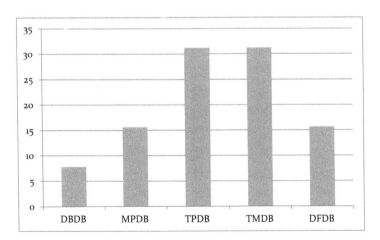

FIG. 3.11 COMPARATIVE IC50 VALUES OF THE COMPOUNDS

CHAPTER- IV

MOLECULAR DOCKING STUDIES AND ANALYSIS

4. INTRODUCTION

Medicinal chemists today are facing a serious challenge because of the increased cost and enormous quantify of time taken to find out a new drug, and additionally due to the fact of rigorous opposition amongst different pharmaceutical companies. Thereby, the significance of computer Aided Drug Design (CADD) and molecular modelling are growing nowadays. Target particular drug discovery is the want of the hour. Advances in computational power, algorithms, and modern database mining methods are accelerating the discovery in science even more. A primary intention in modern drug design is to strengthen new ligands with excessive affinity of binding towards a given protein receptor. Pharmacophore, which is the three-dimensional arrangement of essential features that allow a molecule to exert a unique biological effect, is a very beneficial model for accomplishing this goal. Quantitative Structure-Activity Relationships (QSAR) analyses the correlation between the structural points and the biological activity to predict the activity level of new compounds. Using statistical correlation methods, it builds models to predict the activity level of new compounds. Using statistical correlation methods, it builds models to predict portions such as binding affinity, toxicity, or pharmacokinetic parameters of existing or hypothetical molecules. 3D-QSAR analysis the three-dimensional forces like hydrogen bonds, metal-ligand contacts, polarization impact and the interaction between the electric dipoles. Molecular docking is a nicely established computational approach that predicts the interaction energy between two molecules. This method usually contains algorithms like molecular dynamics, Monte Carlo simulation, and fragment-based search methods. Molecular docking research is used to decide the interaction of two molecules and to find the great orientation of ligand which would form a complicated with general minimum energy. The small molecule recognized as a ligand generally matches within the proteins cavity which is estimated via the search algorithm. These protein cavities become active when they come in contact with any exterior compounds and are thus known as active site. Docking is often used to predict the binding orientation of small molecule drug candidates to their protein targets to predict the affinity and undertaking of the small molecule. Hence docking performs a necessary position in the rational drug design. The effects are analyzed via a statistical scoring characteristic which converts interacting energy into numerical values referred to as the docking score and the glide score is calculated. The 3D pose of the bound ligand can be visualized with the usage of specific visualizing equipment like Pymol, Rasmol, etc, which should help in the inference of the great fit of the ligand. Predicting the mode of protein-ligand interaction can assume the active site of the protein molecule and in addition, assist in protein annotation. Moreover, molecular docking has the most important utility in drug designing and discovery.

4.1 MATERIALS AND METHODS

The 3D crystal structure determination and the structure-activity relationship analysis play a predominant role in designing new drugs to fight against new diseases. AutoDock is an automated procedure for predicting the interaction of ligands with macro molecular targets, using the Lamarckian Genetic Algorithm along with the traditional genetic algorithms and simulated annealing. The empirical free energy scoring function will provide reproducible docking results for ligands with approximately 10 flexible bonds, in addition to, visualizing conformations, visualizing interactions between ligands and proteins, and visualizing the affinity potentials created by AutoGrid. In the present work, the ligand (small molecule)-target (protein) interactions were studied using the AutoDock 4.2.6 software package [141], and the preparation of ligand and protein for the in-silico study and visualizing the interactions between them were done using PyMOL [142] a graphic software. Information regarding the active site interactions can be further used in drug designing and therapy. In this study, the 3D crystal structure of the reference drug complexed with the co-crystal triazole (PDB ID: 3s7s) [143] was downloaded from RCSB Protein Data Bank [144]. After preparing the ligand and protein for molecular docking, the co-crystal inhibitor was replaced by the title compound and the docking processes have initiated with a protein active site dimension of 74x60x62Å grid size along x, y, and z-axis and grid spacing 0.375 Å [145].

4.3 RESULTS AND DISCUSSION
MOLECULAR DOCKING INVESTIGATION
DBDB

Molecular docking analysis has been performed to identify the best pose in which the ligand (small molecule) perfectly fits into the active site of the target (protein) using AutoDock 4.2.6 software and PyMOL graphic software to visualize the molecular interactions. After preparing the ligand and protein for molecular docking, the co-crystal inhibitor was replaced by the title compound and the docking processes initiated with the protein active site of grid spacing 0.375Å. The docking process was continued for ten runs using AutoDock Tools 1.5.6, and the scoring functions including binding energy, inhibition constant, and intermolecular interaction energy was tabulated [Table 4.1].

The protein active site interactions (hydrogen bonding interactions) along with binding energies were given in Table 4.2. The best fit interaction is defined by the lowest binding energy (-9.90 kcal/mol) and the corresponding inhibition constant Ki (0.55μM) [Table 4.1]. In the present work, corresponding to run 2, the ligand interaction with 3s7s protein exhibits the lowest binding energy value of -9.90 kcal/mol, which is illustrative of the excellent binding affinity between the ligand and the protein receptor. Also, the title molecule well fits into the binding site of protein with amino acid residues VAL'370(A) and CYS'437(A) and are in good agreement with the reported co-crystal complexed structure Fig.4.1 [146].

MPDB

The active site interactions between the ligand and the target with PDBID:3s7s is shown in Fig. 4.2. To obtain the best fit interaction defined by the lowest binding energy, 10 runs were tried using AutoDock Tools 1.5.6 and the scoring function's value are tabulated in Table 4.3.The various parameters like binding energy, binding site interactions and donor-acceptor distances were listed in Table 4.4. The inhibition constant (Ki) for the protein (3s7s) with the ligand interaction was found to be 0.7874 (μM), which is the measure of the ligand binding affinity to protein. In the present work, corresponding to run 6, the ligand interaction with 3s7s protein exhibits the lowest binding energy value of -9.69 kcal/mol. The title molecule fits well into the binding site of 3s7s protein and established interactions with amino acid residues VAL'370 and is in good agreement with the reported structures [146].

TPDB

The active site interactions between the ligand and the target with PDBID:3s7s is shown in Fig. 4.3. The interaction is defined by the lowest binding energy, 10 runs were tried using Auto DockTools1.5.6 and the scoring function values are tabulated in Table 4.5. The various parameters like binding energy, binding site interactions and donor-acceptor distances were listed in Table 4.6. The inhibition constant (Ki) for the protein (3s7s) with the ligand interaction was found to be 0.3249 (μM), which is the measure of the ligand binding affinity to protein. In the present work, corresponding to run 8, the ligand interaction with 3s7s protein exhibits the lowest binding energy value of -10.22 kcal/mol. The title molecule fits well into the binding site of 3s7s protein and established interactions with amino acid residues ARG'115 and is in good agreement with the reported structures [146].

TMDB

The active site interactions between the ligand and the target with PDBID:3s7s is shown in Fig.4.4. To obtain the best fit interaction defined by the lowest binding energy, 10 runs were tried using Auto Dock Tools 1.5.6 and the scoring function's value are tabulated in Table 4.7. The various parameters like binding energy, binding site interactions and donor-acceptor distances were listed in Table 4.8. The inhibition constant (Ki) for the protein (3s7s) with the ligand interaction was found to be 0.15963 (μM), which is the measure of the ligand binding affinity to protein. In the present work, corresponding to run 10, the ligand interaction with 3s7s protein exhibits the lowest binding energy value of -9.27 kcal/mol. The title molecules fit well into the binding site of 3s7s protein and established interactions with amino acid residues CYS'437 and are in good agreement with the reported structures [146].

DFDB

The (3E)-3-(2,3-difluoro phenyl) methylidene)-2,3-dihydro-4H-1-benzopyran-4-one (DFDB) molecule used during the docking technique preparation is discontinued, making it impossible to obtain results from the compound.

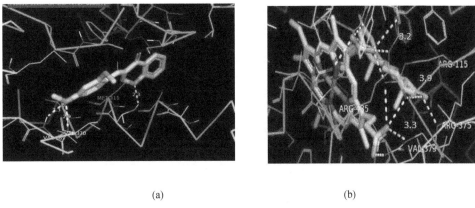

(a)   (b)

FIG.4.1 PYMOL PLOT REPRESENTING THE ACTIVE SITE INTERACTIONS (a) BETWEEN THE LIGAND (DBDB) AND THE PROTEIN (3S7S) (b) BETWEEN THE

CO-CRYSTAL (TRIAZOLE) AND THE PROTEIN (3S7S)

Table 4.1. Scoring functions obtained via molecular docking simulation

Run No.	Binding energy kcal/mol	Inhibition constant (Ki) μM	Intermolecular energy kcal/mol
1	-6.40	0.20	-7.29
2	**-9.90**	**0.55**	**-10.79**
3	-8.01	1.35	-10.02
4	-9.13	2.03	-9.68
5	-8.70	4.22	-9.59
6	-7.59	2.72	-8.49
7	-8.90	2.99	-9.79
8	-7.10	6.28	-7.99
9	-9.17	1.88	-10.07
10	-9.11	2.09	-10.01

Table 4.2. Binding site interactions and binding energies

Ligand	Run No./Pose	Binding site interaction	D-H...A (Å)	Binding energy kcal/mol
Co-crystal (triazole)	5	[VAL'370A)] N-H...O	3.3	-8.70
		[ARG'115(A)] N-H...O	3.9	
		[CYS'437(A)] N-H...O	3.2	
Title molecule (DBDB)	2	[VAL'370(A)] N-H...O	2.3	-9.90

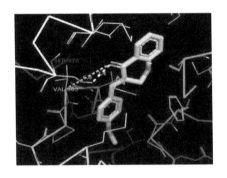 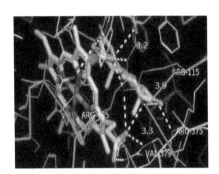

(a)   (b)

**FIG. 4.2 PYMOL PLOT REPRESENTING THE ACTIVE SITE INTERACTIONS
(a) BETWEEN THE LIGAND (MPDB) AND THE PROTEIN (3S7S) (b) BETWEEN THE
CO-CRYSTAL (TRIAZOLE) AND THE PROTEIN (3S7S)**

Table 4.3. Scoring functions obtained via molecular docking simulation

Run No.	Binding energy kcal/mol	Inhibition constant (Ki) μM	Intermolecular energy kcal/mol
1	-9.14	1.99	-9.74
2	-9.09	2.16	-9.69
3	-9.18	1.87	-9.77
4	-9.18	1.85	-9.78
5	-9.20	1.81	-9.79
6	**-9.69**	**0.78**	**-10.29**
7	-9.68	0.77	-10.28
8	-9.06	2.28	-9.66
9	-9.10	2.14	-9.69
10	-9.45	1.18	-10.04

Table 4.4. Binding site interactions and binding energies

Ligand	Run No./Pose	Binding site interaction	D-H...A (Å)	Binding energy kcal/mol
Co-crystal (triazole)	5	[VAL'370A)] N-H...O	3.3	-8.70
		[ARG'115(A)] N-H...O	3.9	
		[CYS'437(A)] N-H...O	3.2	
Title molecule (MPDB)	6	[VAL'370A)] N-H...O	2.4	-9.69

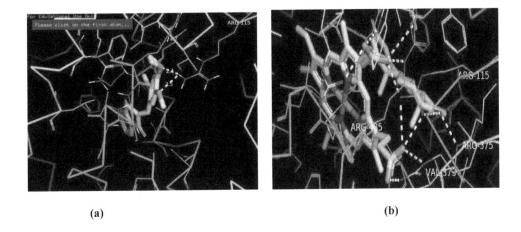

(a)   (b)

FIG. 4.3 PYMOL PLOT REPRESENTING THE ACTIVE SITE INTERACTIONS (a) BETWEEN THE LIGAND (TPDB) AND THE PROTEIN (3S7S) (b) BETWEEN THE CO-CRYSTAL (TRIAZOLE) AND THE PROTEIN (3S7S)

Table 4.5. Scoring functions obtained via molecular docking simulation

Run No.	Binding energy kcal/mol	Inhibition constant (Ki) µM	Intermolecular energy kcal/mol
1	-6.07	0.35	-7.26
2	-8.25	9.01	-9.44
3	-8.72	4.08	-9.91
4	-8.11	1.14	-9.30
5	-8.59	5.06	-9.78
6	-8.71	4.1	-9. 91
7	-10.05	0.4285	-11.2
8	**-10.22**	**0.3249**	**-11.41**
9	-8.98	2.6	-10.17
10	-8.54	5.53	-9.73

Table 4.6. Binding site interactions and binding energies

Ligand	Run No./Pose	Binding site interaction	D-H...A (Å)	Binding energy kcal/mol
Co-crystal (triazole)	5	[VAL'370A)] N-H...O	3.3	-8.70
		[ARG'115(A)] N-H...O	3.9	
		[CYS'437(A)] N-H...O	3.2	
Title molecule (TPDB)	8	[ARG'115] N-H...O	2.5	-10.22

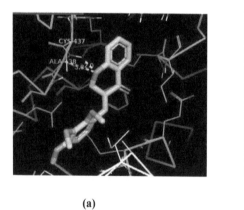

(a)

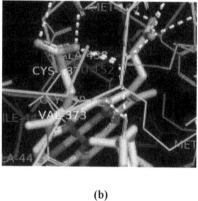

(b)

**FIG. 4.4 PYMOL PLOT REPRESENTING THE ACTIVE SITE INTERACTIONS
(a) BETWEEN THE LIGAND (TMDB) AND THE PROTEIN (3S7S) (b) BETWEEN
THE CO-CRYSTAL (TRIAZOLE) AND THE PROTEIN (3S7S)**

Table 4.7. Scoring functions obtained via molecular docking simulation

Run No.	Binding energy kcal/mol	Inhibition constant(Ki) µM	Intermolecular energy kcal/mol
1	-6.61	0.14	-7.80
2	-9.07	0.22	-10.26
3	-8.31	0.80	-9.50
4	-8.69	0.42	-9.89
5	-8.22	0.93	-9.42
6	-8.98	0.26	-10.17
7	-8.38	0.72	-9.57
8	-7.87	1.71	-9.06
9	-9.10	0.21	-10.29
10	**-9.27**	**0.15**	**-10.47**

Table 4.8. Binding site interactions and binding energies

Ligand	Run No./Pose	Binding site interaction	D-H...A (Å)	Binding energy kcal/mol
Co-crystal (triazole)	6	[VAL'370A)] N-H...O	3.3	
		[ARG'115(A)] N-H...O	3.9	-8.90
		[CYS'437(A)] N-H...O	3.2	
Title molecule (TMDB)	10	[CYS'437(A)] N-H...O	2.0	-9.27

Table 4.9 Comparative analysis of active site interaction of the compounds

Ligand	Run No./Pose	Binding site interaction	D-H...A (Å)	Binding energy kcal/mol
Co-crystal (triazole)	5	[VAL'370A)] N-H...O	3.3	-8.70
		[CYS'310(A)] N-H...O	3.9	
		[ARG'115(A)] N-H...O		
		[CYS'437(A)]N-H...O		
Title molecule DBDB	2	[VAL'370(A)] N-H...O	2.6	-9.90
		[CYS'437(A)] N-H...O	2.9	
MPDB	6	[VAL'370A)] N-H...O	3.1	-9.69
TPDB	8	[ARG'115(A)] N-H...O	2.5	-10.22
TMDB	10	[CYS'310(A)] N-H...O	2.0	-9.27

CHAPTER-V

SPECTRAL, THERMAL, AND MECHANICAL CHARACTERIZATION

OF THE TITLE DERIVATIVES

5. INTRODUCTION

Today's researchers and engineers in the physical and biological sciences have access to an incredible range and powerful tools for collecting qualitative and quantitative information about the composition and structure of matter. Characterization of a substance refers to an exhaustive list of the physical and chemical characteristics of that material. Analyzing the design, optical, mechanical, electrical, and thermal properties of the produced crystals constitute the bulk of characterization. Many characterization techniques focus on the physical and chemical properties of the materials [147]. Due to their many promising uses as chemical probes, electrochromic materials, fluorescent dyes, sensors, additives in dye-sensitized solar cells, and most significantly, in diagnosis for the creation of new medications, fluorescent materials have attracted a lot of attention [148]. Fluorescent chalcones are being utilized to identify several disorders by monitoring changes in emission color in living cells [149]. These luminous chalcones open new applications for non-radioactive replacements [150]. Additionally, new fluorescent chalcone analogs for the inhibition of the formation of β-amyloid plaques, which is the current therapeutic approach used to treat Alzheimer's disease (AD), have been reported [151]. Fluorescent chalcones are advantageous to investigate cellular targets as well as chemical probes for their mechanistic investigations. Another effort was made using heteroaryl chalcones containing both donor and acceptor groups, which improves quantum yields and fluorescence intensity through intermolecular charge transfer (ICT). The use of fluorescence quenching as a crucial metric to study the relationship between bovine serum albumin and derivatives of naphthyl chalcone. The inherent fluorescence properties of chalcones with the proper substituents (electron pull functional groups) on both aryl rings have been described. The main factors in the research of fluorescence are the wavelengths of emission and absorption, the extinction coefficient, and the quantum yield. To display intrinsic fluorescence, these physical properties depend on the electron density across the molecule. According to the results of the previous experimental research, the chalcone needs to have a certain structural property to qualify as a luminous material. Fluorescent property is the emission of electromagnetic radiation of light by a substance that has absorbed ultraviolet radiation of a different wavelength. Many natural and synthetic compounds exhibit fluorescent properties, and they have a wide range of applications.

- Planar molecular structure is required.

- Weak electron-donating groups. Methoxy groups, for example, show higher quantum yields than electron-withdrawing groups, such as nitro and nitrile groups, which show lower quantum yields. The presence of a disubstituted amino group, such as piperazine, piperidine, diethylamino, or dimethyl amino, is extremely significant for the larger emission coefficient, higher quantum yields, and fluorescence with lower ionization potential.
- If the conjugation of the unsaturated system is extended with more bonds, fluorescence will be reduced, which will cause the maximum emission to shift to red.

The grown crystals DBDB, MPDB, TPDB, TMDB, and DFDB were subjected to the following studies.

- Studies using proton and carbon NMR to account for the presence of various protons and carbon atoms in the crystals.
- FT-IR and FT-Raman to investigate the stretching/bending vibrational frequency assignments.
- The UV-Vis spectra to analyze the transmittance capability of the samples in the entire visible region.
- A photoluminescence spectrum to understand the fluorescent property of the compounds.
- TGA/DTA-study the physical and chemical changes due to an increase in temperature hence the thermal properties.
- Microhardness testing estimates the mechanical strength of the materials.

5.1 MATERIALS AND METHODS

All chemicals and solvents used in this study were purchased from Sigma Aldrich and Spectro chem. Pvt Ltd, Chennai, as high purity materials and used as such without any further purification. The grown single crystals were subjected to optical (FTIR, UV-Vis, ^{1}H and ^{13}C NMR and PL), thermal (TG/DTA), mechanical (Vickers hardness test) characterization using the instruments at Sophisticated Analytical Instrumentation Facility (SAIF), IITM, Chennai, Tamilnadu, India. FTIR and FT-RAMAN spectrum was recorded using BRUKER Spectrometer with KBr pellet technique in the range 4000-400cm^{-1} from which the functional groups of the compounds have been assigned with vibration (stretching/bending) frequencies. The proton and carbon NMR spectra of the compounds were recorded using Bruker Advance III 400 MHz Spectrometer and CDCl$_3$ as a solvent and the chemical shift for the equivalent protons/carbons with different chemical environments were analyzed. The absorption spectrum was recorded in the wavelength range of 200-800nm using Carry 100 UV/Vis spectrometer. The photoluminescence study (PL) of the compounds was carried out using the Perkin Elmer-Ls 45 luminescence spectrometer in the range of 400-800nm. Simultaneous Thermogravimetric analysis (TGA) and Differential thermal analysis (DTA) were carried out under a nitrogen atmosphere using a NETZSCH STA 409PC/PG thermal analyzer available at St. Joseph's College, Tiruchirappalli in Tamil Nadu, India. Mechanical properties of the synthesized compounds were studied by the Vickers method which is based on an optical measurement system, and specifies a range of light loads using an indenter to make an indentation which is measured and converted to a hardness value.

5.2 RESULTS AND DISCUSSION

A mixture of NaOH (10%, 10 mL), and benzaldehyde derivatives was stirred at 2h and left in the refrigerator overnight. The precipitated solid was then filtered off, washed with water and ethanol, dried, and crystallized from ethanol to yield yellow crystals

5.2.1 PROTON AND CARBON NMR SPECTRAL STUDIES

DBDB

(3E)-3-(2,4-dimethoxyphenyl) methylidene)-2,3-dihydro-4H-1-benzopyran one
(Fig. 5.1): Yellow color single crystal, yield 85%,m.p.: 98°C, $C_{18}H_{16}O_4$, ^1HNMR (δ in ppm, CDCl$_3$, 500MHz): 6.49-8.03 (m, 7H, Ar-H), 3.84(m, 6H, O-CH$_3$), 1.87 (m, 2H, CH$_2$), Conjugated (m, H, 5.24).^{13}C-NMR (δ in ppm, CDCl$_3$, 500MHz) 182.45 (C=O), 98.51-162.57 (Ar-C), 131.54-135.49 (C=C), 68.25-77.33 (O-CH$_3$), 55.50-55.55 (CH$_2$) [152].

MPDB

(3E)-3-(4-methoxyphenyl) methylidene)-2,3-dihydro-4H-1-benzopyran-4-one
(Fig. 5.1): Yellow crystal, yield 95%, m.p.: 102°C, $C_{17}H_{14}O_3$, ^{1}H-NMR (δ in ppm, CDCl$_3$,500MHz): 6.94-8.02 (m, 7H, Ar-H), 3.85(m, 3H, O-CH$_3$), 1.78 (m, 2H, CH$_2$), Conjugated (m, H, 5.36). ^{13}C-NMR (δ in ppm, CDCl$_3$, 500MHz) 182.15 (C=O), 114.28-160.97 (Ar-C), 132.07-137.30 (C=C), 76.82-77.33 (O-CH$_3$), 55.41(CH$_2$) [152].

TPDB

(3E)-3-(2,4,5-trimethoxyphenyl) methylidene) -2,3-dihydro-4H-1-benzopyran-4-one
(Fig. 5.2): Yellow crystal, yield 85%, m.p.:70°C, $C_{19}H_{18}O_5$, ^{1}H-NMR (δ in ppm, CDCl$_3$, 500MHz): 6.50-8.03 (m, 7H, Ar-H), 3.85 (m, 9H, O-CH$_3$), 1.87 (m, 2H, CH$_2$), Conjugated (m, H, 5.24). ^{13}C-NMR (δ in ppm, CDCl$_3$, 500MHz) 187.98 (C=O), 96.06-161.16 (Ar-C), 133.54-135.64 (C=C), 76.80 -77.31 (O-CH$_3$), 56.10 (CH$_2$) [153].

TMDB

(3E)-3-(2,3,4-trimethoxyphenyl) methylidene) -2,3-dihydro-4H-1-benzopyran-4-one
(Fig. 5.2): Yellow crystal, yield 83%, m.p.: 75°C, $C_{19}H_{18}O_5$, ^{1}H-NMR (δ in ppm, CDCl$_3$,

141

500MHz): 6.70-8.04 (m, 7H, Ar-H), 3.87 (m, 9H, O-CH$_3$), 1.68 (m, 2H, CH$_2$), Conjugated (m, H, 5.23). ^{13}C-NMR (δ in ppm, CDCl$_3$, 500MHz) 182.43 (C=O), 106.48-161.17 (Ar-C), 133.16 - 135.48 (C=C), 65.26-77.35 (O-CH$_3$), 56.11(CH$_2$) [152].

DFDB

(3E)-3-(2,3-difluorophenyl) methylidene) -2,3-dihydro-4H-1-benzopyran-4-one
(Fig. 5.3): Yellow crystal, yield 95%, m.p.: 137°C, C$_{16}$H$_{10}$F$_2$O$_2$, ^{1}H-NMR (δ in ppm, CDCl$_3$, 500MHz): 6.53-8.04 (m, 7H, Ar-H), 1.64 (m, 2H, CH$_2$), Conjugated (m, H, 5.41). ^{13}C-NMR (δ in ppm, CDCl$_3$, 500MHz) 182.01 (C=O), 116.03-161.40 (Ar-C), 133.08-136.11 (C=C), 54.43(CH$_2$) [153].

5.2.2 FT-IR AND FT-RAMAN SPECTRAL ANALYSIS
DBDB

The absorbance signals in the recorded FT-IR spectrum of the compound DBDB (Fig.5.4) have been assigned with wave numbers as follows: [(str./bending, the intensity of the peak, and wave number cm^{-1})]: aromatic C-H (str., w, 3037), CH$_3$,CH$_2$/C-H (str., m, 2835, 2905,2957), C=O (str., s, 1685), C=C aromatic (str., s, 1599), C-O (str., s, 1011-1323), C-C (str., m, 1416-1508), asymmetric C-O-C (str., s, 1210,1247), C–H out of the plane (ben., s, 621-748), Aromatic C-C deformation (ben., s, 531). The absorbance bands associated with the functional groups present in DBDB are found to be within the expected range and the assigned wave number values are in good agreement with the reported values [154,155].

The FT-RAMAN spectra for all the synthesized compounds were recorded in the frequency range of 100 - 4000 cm^{-1}. The recorded FT-RAMAN spectrum of the compound DBDB (Fig.5.4) has been assigned with wave numbers as follows: [(str./bending, intensity of the peak, and wave number cm^{-1})]: aromatic C-H (str., w, 3012, 3065), CH$_3$,CH$_2$/C-H (str., m, 2842, 2945),C=O (str., w, 1664), C=C aromatic (str., s, 1587), C-C (str., m, 1315), asymmetric C-O-C (str., s, 1213-1280), symmetric C-O (str., m, 1029-1158), C–H out of the plane (ben., m,705), aromatic C-C deformation (ben., s, 501) [156].

MPDB

The FT-IR spectrum of the compound MPDB (Fig. 5.5) has been assigned with wave numbers as follows: [(str./bending, intensity of the peak, and wave number cm^{-1})]: aromatic   C-H (str., w, 3008, 3071), CH$_3$,CH$_2$/C-H (str., m, 2835, 2941, 2967),C=O (str., s, 1659), C=C aromatic (str., s, 1584), C-O (str., s, 1020-1309), C-C (str., m, 1458-1501), asymmetric C-O-C (str., s, 1205,1263), C-H out of the plane (ben., s, 632-781),aromatic C-C deformation(ben., s, 535,571) [154,155].

The recorded FT-RAMAN spectrum of the compound MPDB has been assigned with wave numbers as follows: [(str./bending, intensity of the peak and wave   number   cm^{-1})]: aromatic C-H (str., m, 3002 & 3070), CH$_3$,CH$_2$/C-H (str., m, 2845, 2977), C=O (str., w, 1664), C=C aromatic (str., s, 1596),   C-C (str., m, 1307), asymmetric C-O-C (str., s, 1210-1250), symmetric C-O (str., m, 1032-1174), C-H out of the plane (ben., m, 826), aromatic C-C deformation (ben., s. 490) [156].

TMDB

The recorded FT-IR spectrum of the compound TPDB (Fig. 5.6) has been assigned with wave numbers as follows: [(str./bending, intensity of the peak, and wave number   cm^{-1})]: aromatic C-H (str., w, 3001, 3006), CH$_3$,CH$_2$/C-H (str., m, 2835, 2861, 2934, 2964), hydrogen-bonded OH (str., w, 3429, 3564), C=O (str., s, 1662), C=C aromatic (str., s, 1513), C-O (str., s, 1010-1290), C-C (str., m, 1406-1513), asymmetric C-O-C (str., s, 1212,1266),   C-H out of plane (629-788), aromatic C-C deformation (ben., s, 509, 578) [154,155].

The FT-RAMAN spectrum of the compound TPDB has been assigned with wave numbers as follows: [(str./bending, intensity of the peak and wave number cm^{-1})]: aromatic   C-H (str., w, 3066), CH$_3$,CH$_2$/C-H (str., m, 2840, 2940), C=O (str., w, 1660), C=C aromatic (str., s, 1513), C-C (str., s, 1340), asymmetric C-O-C (str., s, 1246,1288), symmetric C-O (ben., m, 1032,1161), C-H out of the plane (ben., m,757), aromatic C-C deformation (ben., m, 502) [156].

TMDB

The recorded FT-IR spectrum of the compound TMDB (Fig. 5.7) has been assigned with wave numbers as follows: [(str./bending, intensity of the peak, and wave number cm^{-1})]: aromatic C-H (str., w, 3101, 3069), CH$_3$,CH$_2$/C-H (str., m, 2840, 2938, 2966), hydrogen-bonded OH (str., w, 3435), C=O (str., s, 1668), C=C aromatic (str., s, 1597), C-O (str., s, 1001-1267), C-C (str., s, 1413-1597), asymmetric C-O-C (str., s, 1220), C–H out of a plane (ben., s, 672-781), aromatic C-C deformation (ben., s, 521-599) [154,155].

The FT-RAMAN spectrum of the compound TMDB has been assigned with wave numbers as follows: [(str./bending, intensity of the peak and wave number cm^{-1})]: aromatic   C-H (str., w, 3129), CH$_3$,CH$_2$/C-H (str., m, 2804, 2873, 2918, 2935), C=O (str., w, 1644), C=C aromatic (str., s, 1480), C-C (str., s, 1299), asymmetric C-O-C (str., s, 1246, 1288), C-O (ben., m, 1048,1085), C-H out of the plane (ben., m, 659) [156].

DFDB

The FT-IR spectrum of the compound DFDB (Fig.5.8) has been assigned with wave numbers as follows: [(str./bending, intensity of the peak, and wave number cm^{-1})]: aromatic   C-H (str., w, 3080), CH$_2$/C-H (str., m, 2916), C=O (str., s, 1675), C=C aromatic (str., s, 1584), C-O (str., s, 1003-1299), C-C (str., s, 1384-1473), asymmetric C-O-C (str., s, 1217,1276), C-H out of a plane (ben., s, 623-793), aromatic C-C deformation(ben., s, 529,565).

The FT-RAMAN spectrum of the compound DFDB (Fig.5.8) has been assigned with wave numbers as follows:[(str./bending, intensity of the peak and, wave number   cm^{-1})]: aromatic C-H (str., w, 3016-3080), CH$_2$/C-H (str., m, 2910, 2980),C=O (str., w, 1675), C=C aromatic (str., s, 1587), C-C (str., s, 1315), asymmetric C-O-C (str., s, 1218,1290), symmetric C-O (ben., m, 1033, 1151), C-H out of a plane (ben., m,759), aromatic C-C deformation (ben., m, 566).

5.2.3 UV-VIS. SPECTRAL STUDIES OF TITLE COMPOUNDS

DBDB

The absorption spectrum of DBDB shown in Fig. 5.12, containing peaks at 259, 374nm is attributed to $\pi \rightarrow \pi^*$ transition due to the carbonyl group. The absence of an absorption peak anywhere between 450 - 800nm demonstrates the wide transparency over the entire visible region, hence must be a good material for optoelectronic applications [157]. From the recorded spectrum, the cut-off wavelength of the grown crystal is measured as λc = 450 nm and the band gap is calculated using the formula,

$$E_g = \frac{12.4237}{\lambda c} \; eV \text{--------- [1]}$$

The calculated band gap value of the DBDB crystal is 2.760 eV.

MPDB

The absorption spectrum of MPDB is shown in Fig. 5.12. The charge transfer excitation at 351nm is ascribed to the π π^* transition and may be due to the C=O group. The cut-off wavelength of the grown crystal is λc =420 nm and the calculated band gap using the equation [1] is 2.958 eV.

TPDB

The recorded UV-Visible spectrum of grown crystal is shown in Fig.5.13. The optical absorption study shows that the UV cut-off wavelength of TPDB occurs at 295 nm. Itis well known that the efficient NLO crystal has optical transparency at alower cut-off wavelength of 400 nm. The peaks at 210, 238, 270, and 350nm in the recorded spectrum of the grown crystal are due to the $\pi \pi^*$ and those might be due to the presence of C= O moiety. The band gap energy is 3.105 eV using the equation [1] with the cut-off wavelength λc = 400 nm.

TMDB

The optical absorption spectrum for the grown crystal has been recorded in the range between 200 to 800 nm and is shown in Fig.5.13. The grown crystal has UV cut off below 300 nm and above which the grown crystal is transparent in the entire visible range of the spectrum which has good agreement with the literature. The peaks at 230, 270 and 330 nm are due to the π π^* transitions associated with the C= O. The band gap energy is 3.105 eV using the equation [1] with the wavelength $\lambda c = 400$ nm.

DFDB

The recorded absorption spectrum of the compound Fig. 5.13 reveals that the cut-off wavelength is around 420 nm and the absorption peak is at 340nm in the UV region. The π π^* electronic transitions at 277nm are related to the carbonyl group (C=O). The band gap energy is 2.958 eV [λc = 420nm] by using the formula in the equation [1]. The absorption peak, band gap energy and cut-off wavelength values of the grown compounds are listed in Table 5.4.

5.2.4 PHOTOLUMINESCENCE SPECTRAL ANALYSIS OF TITLE COMPOUNDS

The emission spectral analysis of the synthesized compounds at room temperature and the recorded spectrum of the compounds DBDB, MPDB, TPDB, TMDB, and DFDB were shown in Fig. 5.14-5.15, respectively.

The emission spectrum of the compound DBDB is with an excitation peak at 374nm and emission wavelength at 450nm, which indicates blue light emission. Similarly, the spectrum of the compounds MPDB, TPDB, TMDB, and DFDB have strong and broad level emissions at 420, 481, 480, and 414nm with excitation at 351, 345, 399 and 397nm, respectively. These emission wavelengths are corresponding to blue emissions accordingly. In addition, this blue light emission indicates π-electron mobility from donor to acceptor groups in the compounds [158]. The broad emission spectrum of all compounds was indicating a greater number of different vibration levels in excited states [159].

5.2.6 THERMAL STUDIES OF TITLECOMPOUNDS
DBDB

TG/DTA thermograms of the title compound were carried out under nitrogen atmosphere conditions between 0-800°C. In compound DBDB, the DTA (Fig. 5.16) thermogram shows two prominent endothermic peaks at 135.72 and 326.47°C. In the TG curve, the first weight loss is observed between 98-170°C. The heavyweight loss was observed between 280-340°C leaving a residual mass of 0.1934 mg. The minimum weight loss of about 2.305% is observed around 380-780°C. Thermal analysis shows that the title compound is thermally stable up to 238°C.

MPDB

Fig. 5.16 represents the TG/DTA thermograms of the title compound MPDB. TG curve shows simple degradation with the residual mass of about 0.01590mg. In the DTA trace, a sharp endothermic peak at 136.76°C is followed by another endothermic peak at 307.64°C. These two endothermic peaks are corresponding to the melting processes and decomposition of ethylene (CH_2) and carbonyl ($C=O$) groups liberation from the title compound [160]. There is no trace of peaks observed before 136.76°C, which indicates the purity of the sample, and the compound can be thermally stable up to 230°C.

TPDB

In compound TPDB, the recorded TG/ DTA curves are shown in Fig.5.17, from the mass decay occurs a single step leaving a residual mass of 0.1616mg. First weight loss was initially observed between 60-160°C. In the DTA trace a sharp endothermic peak at 94.60°C.These endothermic peaks are corresponding to the melting processes and decomposition of ethylene (CH_2) and carbonyl ($C=O$) groups liberation from the title compound [160]. The compound can be thermally stable up to 220°C.

TMDB

In compound TMDB, the TG/DTA thermogram (Fig. 5.17) shows endothermic (DTA) with a sharp peak occurring at 112.11°C, which is immediately followed by another endothermic peak at 287.70°C. The first endothermic peak represents the melting point and the second peak attributes to the initial stage decomposition of the compound. The compound can be thermally stable up to 230°C.

DFDB

Fig. 5.17 corresponds to TG/ DTA curves of compound DFDB, according to the TG curve, the mass losses take processes from 40-220°C. A sharp endothermic peak at 130.06°C is attributed to the melting point of the compound. Another peak appeared at 271.86°C. In this step, organic compound is propagated by combustion. After the oxidation process, the residual mass available is 10.86% at 800°C. The compound can be thermally stable up to 210°C.

5.2.7 VICKERS MICROHARDNESS TEST

As the hardness properties are related to the crystal structure of the material, microhardness studies have been carried out to understand the plasticity of the crystals. The higher hardness value for all grown crystals indicates greater stress required to form dislocation which confirms greater crystalline perfection. The highest values of hardness were found to be 69.8, 44.75, 45.1, 62.6, 98.95 kg/mm^2 for the compounds DBDB,MPDB,TPDB,TMDB and DFDB, respectively, at the load of

100g. The graph is plotted between the load and the hardness values for the grown compounds are shown in Fig.5.18. H_V should increase with the increase of load, if n > 2, and decrease if n < 2. 'n' lies between 1.0 and 1.6 for hard materials and more than 1.6 for soft materials. Fig. 5.19 shows the plot of log d Vs log P for the grown compounds and the Mayer's index (n)is found to be 3.058, 2.318, 2.649, 3.32, and 4.83 for the compounds DBDB, MPDB, TPDB, TMDB, and DFDB, respectively, which reveals that the synthesized materials are belonging to soft material.

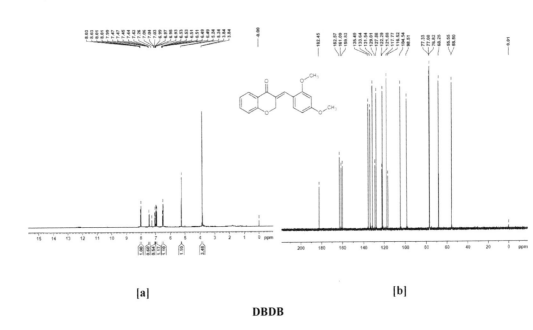

[a]   [b]

DBDB

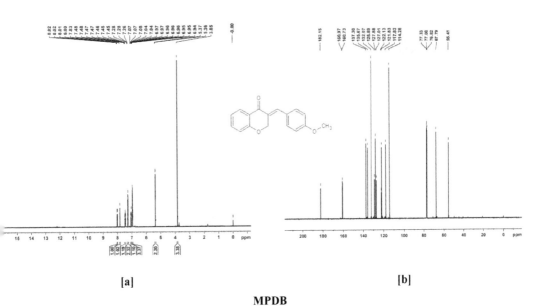

[a]   [b]

MPDB

FIG.5.1. [a] PROTON AND [b] CARBON NMR SPECTRA

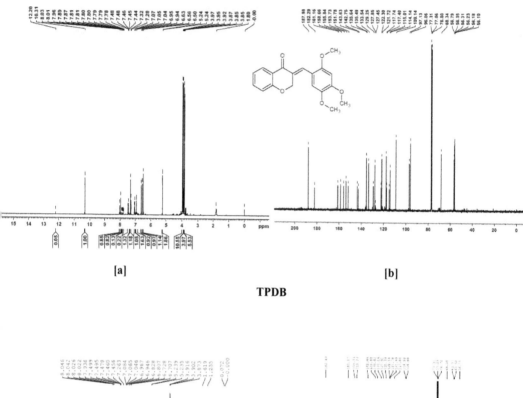

[a]

[b]

TPDB

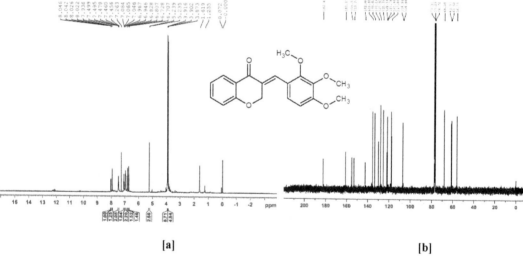

[a]

[b]

TMDB

FIG.5.2. [a] PROTON AND [b] CARBON NMR SPECTRA

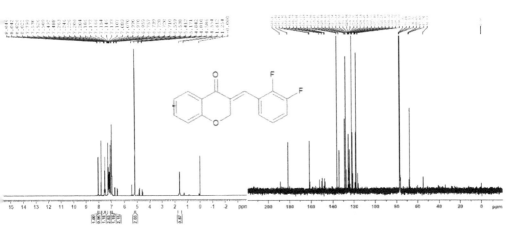

[a]   [b]

DFDB

FIG.5.3. [a] PROTON AND [b] CARBON NMR SPECTRA

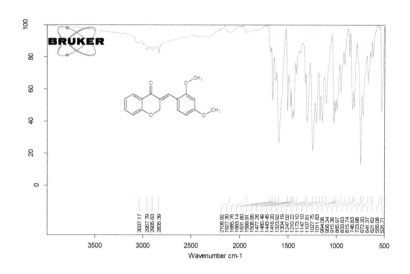

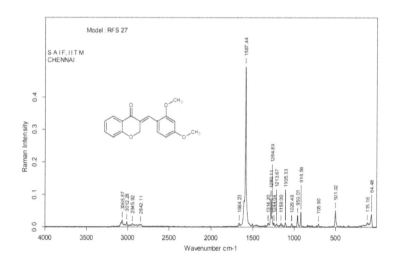

FIG.5.4. FT- IR AND FT-RAMAN SPECTRA - DBDB

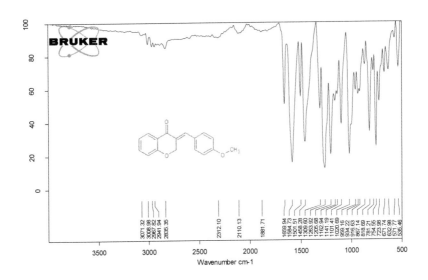

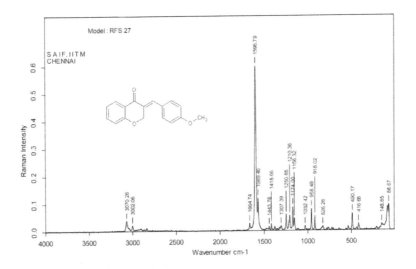

FIG.5.5. FT- IR AND FT-RAMAN SPECTRA - MPDB

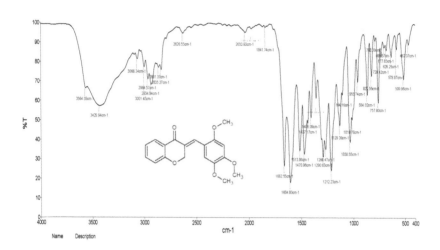

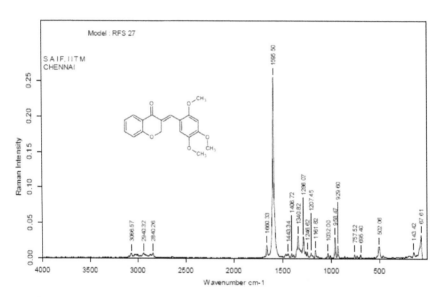

FIG.5.6. FT- IR AND FT-RAMAN SPECTRA - TPDB

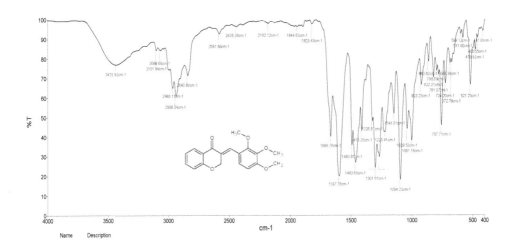

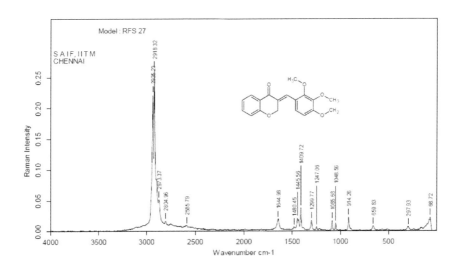

FIG.5.7. FT- IR AND FT-RAMAN SPECTRA – TMDB

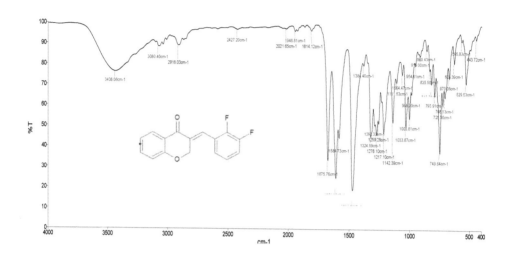

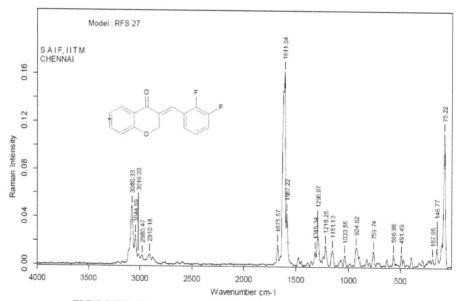

FIG.5.8. FT- IR AND FT-RAMAN SPECTRA - DFDB

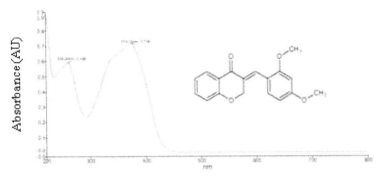

DBDB

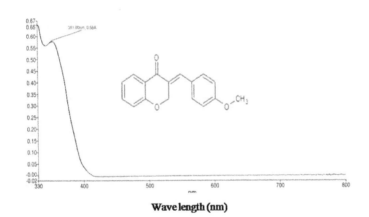

MPDB

FIG.5.12. UV- VISIBLE SPECTRA

156

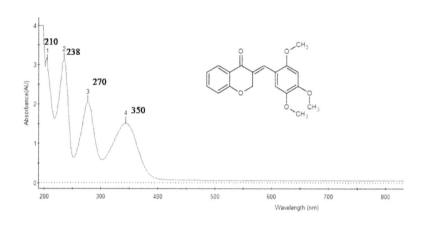

TPDB

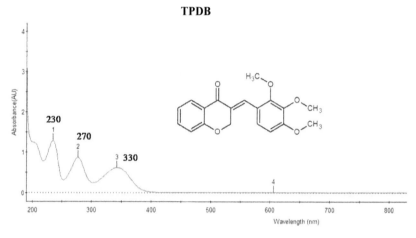

TMDB

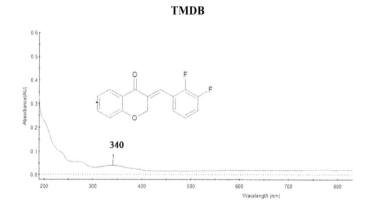

DFDB FIG.5.13. UV- VISIBLE SPECTRA

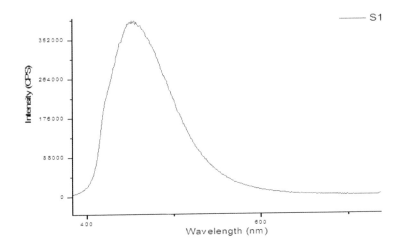

DBDB

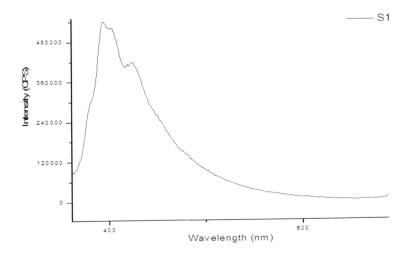

MPDB

FIG.5.14. EMISSION SPECTRA

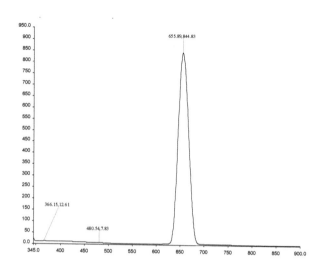

TPDB

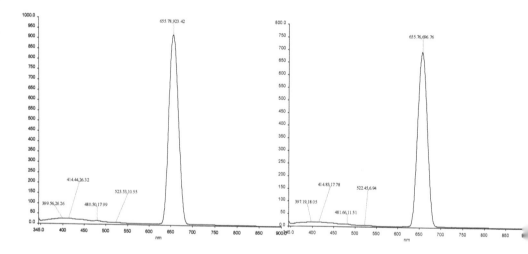

TMDB

DFDB

FIG.5.15. EMISSION SPECTRA

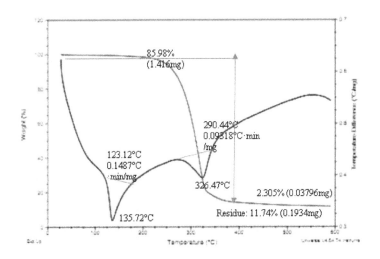

DBDB

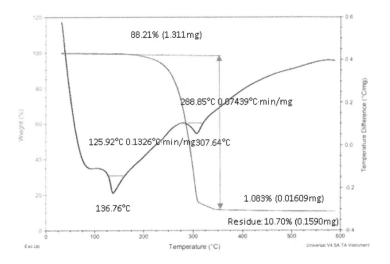

MPDB

FIG.5.16. TG/ DTA THERMOGRAMS

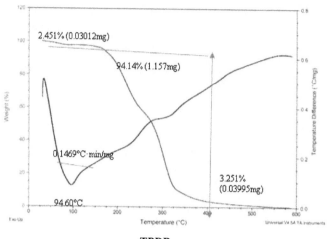

TPDB

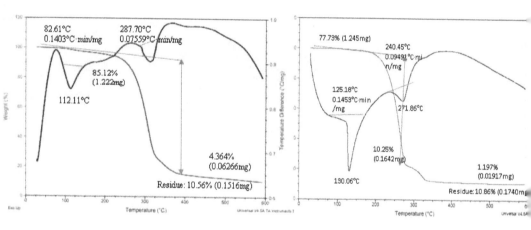

TMDB

DFDB

FIG.5.17. TG/ DTA THERMOGRAMS

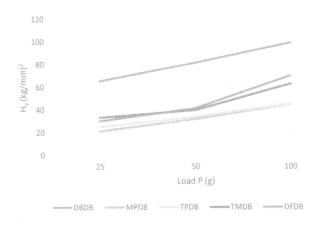

FIG. 5.18 VICKERS HARDNESS GRAPH PLOTTED BETWEEN LOAD AND HARDNESS VALUES

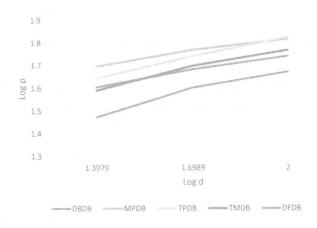

FIG. 5.19 THE PLOT OF log d VS log p

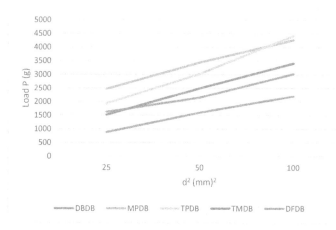

FIG.5.20 THE PLOT BETWEEN d² and Load p

Table 5.1 $_1H^1$ Spectral Studies

Hydrogen type	DBDB	MPDB	TPDB	TMDB	DFDB	Reference
	Chemical Shift (ppm)					(ppm)
Aromatic C-H	6.49-8.03	6.94-8.02	6.50-8.03	6.70-8.04	6.53-8.04	6.4-8.2
CH$_3$	3.84	3.85	3.85	3.87	-	2.07-3.89
CH$_2$	1.87	1.78	1.87	1.68	1.64	1-2
Conjugated H	5.24	5.36	5.24	5.23	5.41	5.1-5.9

Table 5.2 ^{13}C Spectral Studies

Carbon type	DBDB	MPDB	TPDB	TMDB	DFDB	Reference
	Chemical Shift (ppm)					(ppm)
Carbonyl ester C=O	182.45	182.15	187.98	182.43	182.01	195-220
Ar-C	98.51-162.57	114.28-160.97	96.06-161.16	106.48-161.17	116.03-161.40	110-170
C=C	131.54-135.49	132.07-137.30	133.54-135.64	133.16-135.48	133.08-136.11	120-140
O-CH$_3$	68.25-77.33	76.82-77.33	76.80-77.31	65.26-77.35	-	50 -90
CH$_2$	55.50-55.55	55.41	56.10	56.11	54.43	15-55

Table 5.4 Cut-off wavelength, Band gap energy for the compounds

Compounds	Cut-off wavelength(nm)	Band gap energy (eV)
DBDB	450	2.760
MPDB	420	2.958
TPDB	400	3.105
TMDB	400	3.105
DFDB	420	2.958

Table 5.5 Emission peak of the compounds

Compounds	Emission peak (nm)
DBDB	450
MPDB	430
TPDB	480,657
TMDB	523,655
DFDB	481,656

Table 5.6 Calculated values of Microhardness test

Compounds	Load P (g)	d (mm)	H_v (kg/mm^2)	Work hardening coefficient ' n'
DBDB	25	38.61	30.05	3.058
	50	45.48	41.45	
	100	53.82	69.8	
MPDB	25	47.65	21.2	2.318
	50	55.61	31.8	
	100	64.625	44.75	
TMDB	25	42.8	24.9	2.649
	50	53.78	33.8	
	100	64.84	45.1	
TPDB	25	37.72	33.15	3.32
	50	47.85	39.7	
	100	55.59	62.6	
DFDB	25	28.26	65.15	4.83
	50	37.8	81.35	
	100	44.64	98.95	

CPSIA information can be obtained
at www.ICGtesting.com
Printed in the USA
LVHW020647250423
745210LV00009B/380

9 781805 270317